HOME DESIGNS
for family living

Home Designs For Family Living is a collection of our best-selling home plans featured in a variety of styles and sizes all perfect for family living. A broad assortment is presented to match a wide variety of lifestyles and budgets. Each design page features floor plans, a front view of the house, interior square footage of the home, number of bedrooms, baths, garage size and foundation types. All floor plans show room and exterior dimensions. Each plan page offers a comprehensive look at a beautiful home designed with family living in mind. Whether you are looking for large bedrooms, multiple baths, an expansive kitchen or plenty of outdoor living spaces, this collection of home plans won't disappoint you. So, keeping your families' needs in mind, browse through this collection of plans and look for your family's dream home. We are sure it can be found amidst the home plans offered in this book. Your dream home is definitely within reach.

COVER HOME - The house shown on the front cover is
Plan #587-051D-0186 and is featured on page 37.
Photo courtesy of Ahmann Designs, Inc., Hiawatha, IA.

HOME DESIGNS FOR FAMILY LIVING - HOME PLANS
is published by HDA, Inc. (Home Design Alternatives) 944 Anglum Road,
St. Louis, MO, 63042. All rights reserved. Reproduction in whole or in
part without written permission of the publisher is prohibited. Printed in
U.S.A. © 2006. Artist drawings and photos shown in this publication may
vary slightly from the actual working drawings. Some photos are shown
in mirror reverse. Please refer to the floor plan for accurate layout.

Current Printing

10 9 8 7 6 5 4 3 2 1

HDA, Inc. (Home Design Alternatives)
944 Anglum Rd.
St. Louis, Missouri 63042
corporate website - www.hdainc.com
www.houseplansandmore.com

CONTENTS

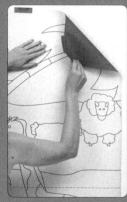

HOME DESIGNS
for family living

A house becomes a home when filled with people. Whether those in your home are visiting friends or rambunctious children, there is a home design in this collection to fulfill your wants and needs. Designed with family in mind, each plan ensures an easy flow of activities.

Imagine catching up with your children's day while you cook dinner and they sit and relax at the large island snack bar. Imagine curling up to a good book in your cozy living room while your teenagers play games with friends on the lower level. Imagine hosting a summer barbecue with your grand outdoor living space.

Finding a home using smart and efficient design creates a comfortable way of life, even amongst the most luxurious amenities. Whatever your family desires, from intimate gatherings to formal affairs, there is a plan for you.

We invite you to browse through our collection of plans designed for family living. Among these pages, we're sure you will find your family's dream home.

Photos from top: 587-024D-0008, page 46; 587-065D-0087, page 14;
587-052D-0115, page 64; 587-065D-0013, page 90

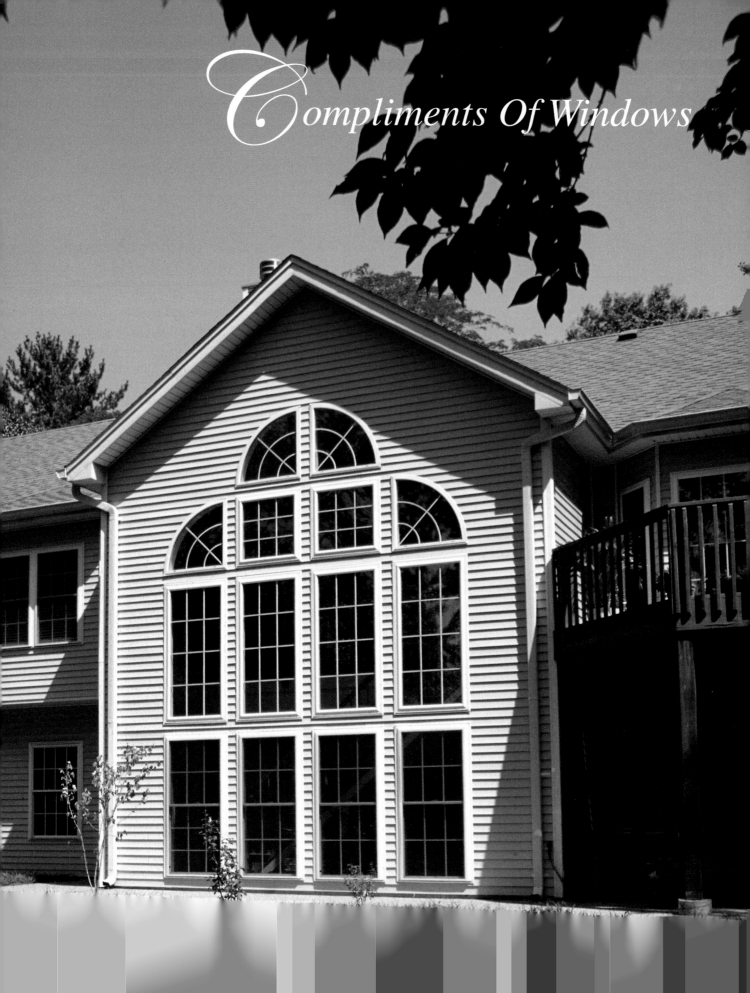

Compliments Of Windows

Total Square Feet - 1,721

Bedrooms - 3

Baths - 2

Garage - 3-car

Foundation - Walk-out basement, drawings also include crawl space and slab

Roof dormers add great curb appeal to the exterior while vaulted dining and great rooms are immersed in light from the atrium window wall. A sunny breakfast room opens onto the covered porch with a functionally designed kitchen nearby. This home features 1,604 square feet on the first floor and 117 square feet on the lower level atrium making it the perfect home for any family.

Price Code C

Rear View

*W*arm Cozy Surroundings

Total Square Feet - 1,793
Bedrooms - 3
Baths - 2
Garage - 2-car side entry

Foundation - Basement, crawl space
or slab, please specify when ordering

A beautiful foyer leads into the great
room of this home that features
a fireplace flanked by two sets of
beautifully transomed doors both
leading to a large covered porch.
Nearby a dramatic eat-in kitchen
includes an abundance of cabinets
and workspace in an exciting angled
shape. The delightful master bedroom
is loaded with many amenities
making it perfect for quiet times.
Plus, an optional bonus room above
the garage has an additional 779
square feet of living area
perfect for a growing family.

Price Code B

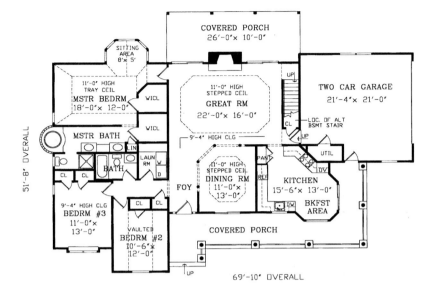

$\mathcal{R}$ambling Ranch Is Filled Sunlight

Total Square Feet -2,523

Bedrooms - 3

Baths - 2

Garage - 3-car

Foundation - Basement

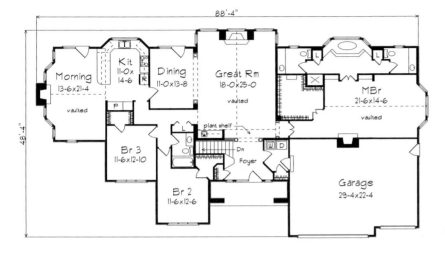

Welcoming and inviting, the entry greets guests with a high ceiling leading to a massive vaulted great room with wet bar, plant shelves, pillars and fireplace with a harmonious window trio. Nearby, an elaborate kitchen with bay and breakfast bar adjoins a morning room with a fireplace-in-a-bay. All living areas are filled with extras to make an unforgettable impression. Even more areas offer special touches, including the vaulted master bedroom. In this retreat you'll find a fireplace, book and plant shelves, a large walk-in closet and double baths offering the ultimate in pampering and luxury living.

Price Code D

Exciting Rooms

Second Floor - 349 sq. ft.

GAME ROOM
22'-2" X 14'-6"

Total Square Feet - 2,755

Bedrooms - 4

Baths - 4

Garage - 3-car side entry

Foundation - Slab, crawl space,
basement or walk-out basement,
please specify when ordering

*The breakfast room of this home
boasts a two-story vaulted ceiling
adding an immense amount of
spaciousness to this family gathering
area. Just beyond, step onto the 10'
covered porch which has enough
space for eating outdoors or just
relaxing in the refreshing breeze.
In addition, each bedroom is lucky
enough to have its own private bath.
This is definitely a terrific layout for
families with children of all ages.*

Price Code E

First Floor - 2,406 sq. ft.

Stylish Two-Story

Second Floor - 986 sq. ft.

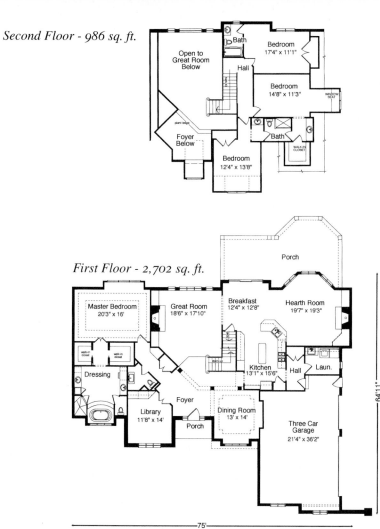

Plan #587-065D-0087

Total Square Feet - 3,688
Bedrooms - 4
Baths - 3 1/2
Garage - 3-car side entry
Foundation - Basement

Formal and informal areas provide space for various social events and comfortable family living throughout this home. A gourmet kitchen with open bar and island serves the dining room and breakfast area with equal ease. A secluded hall creates an orderly transition from the kitchen to the laundry and garage. Furthermore, a wonderful master bedroom is decorated by a stepped ceiling, crown molding, a boxed window and a lavish bath with a platform whirlpool tub just waiting to pamper.

Price Code F

First Floor - 2,702 sq. ft.

Simple Elegance Achieved

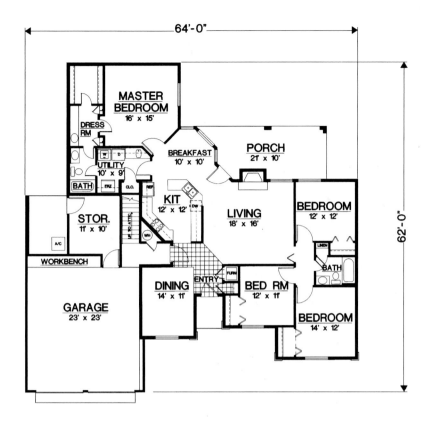

Plan #587-020D-0007

Total Square Feet - 1,828

Bedrooms - 4

Baths - 2

Garage - 2-car

Foundation - Slab foundation, drawings also include crawl space and basement

Designed with style and beauty from the inside out, this home is also designed to be energy efficient with 2" x 6" exterior walls perfect for maintaining economical heating and cooling costs year-round. In addition to its great function, high style is created with a master bath featuring a giant walk-in closet and built-in linen storage with convenient access to the utility room. Plus, the kitchen has a unique design that is elegant and practical, no doubt becoming the center of activity.

Price Code C

Oversized Rooms With An Efficient Design

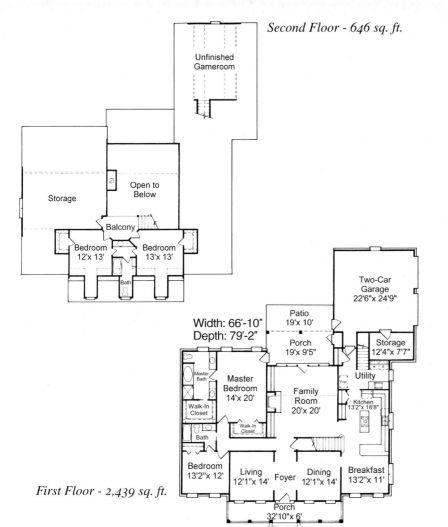

Second Floor - 646 sq. ft.

Unfinished Gameroom

Storage

Open to Below

Balcony

Bedroom 12'x 13'

Bedroom 13'x 13'

Bath

Width: 66'-10"
Depth: 79'-2"

First Floor - 2,439 sq. ft.

Two-Car Garage 22'6"x 24'9"

Patio 19'x 10'

Porch 19'x 9'5"

Storage 12'4"x 7'7"

Utility

Master Bath

Master Bedroom 14'x 20'

Walk-In Closet

Bath

Family Room 20'x 20'

Walk-In Closet

Kitchen 13'2"x 18'8"

Bedroom 13'2"x 12'

Living 12'1"x 14'

Foyer

Dining 12'1"x 14'

Breakfast 13'2"x 11'

Porch 32'10"x 6'

Plan #587-024D-0056

Total Square Feet - 3,085

Bedrooms - 4

Baths - 3

Garage - 2-car side entry

Foundation - Slab, crawl space or basement, please specify when ordering

This home has a wonderful family room featuring a two-story ceiling, full wall of windows and a raised hearth fireplace flanked by built-in bookshelves. The family chef is sure to enjoy the kitchen with a cooktop island and snack bar that opens to the breakfast area. The unfinished gameroom has an additional 180 square feet of living area ideal for socializing or casual family relaxation.

Price Code G

Home Has A Contemporary Feel

Optional Second Floor - 849 sq. ft.

Bonus Rm.
18'⁷ • 15'⁵

Bath

Study Niche
9'¹ • 7'¹

Office
11'⁶ • 13'¹

Mech.

Plan #587-047D-0052

Total Square Feet - 3,098

Bedrooms - 4

Baths - 4

Garage - 3-car side entry

Foundation - Slab

Luxury and lavish surroundings are found in every corner of this home. The master bedroom is elegant with a private bath, an enormous walk-in closet and a sitting area leading to the lanai. The vaulted family room has plenty of windows and a cozy corner fireplace. Or, enjoy a secluded study with double closets and built-ins offering a more, intimate environment if desired. Please note that only concrete block framing is available for this home.

Price Code F

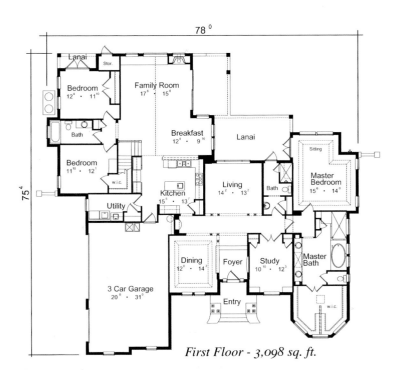

First Floor - 3,098 sq. ft.

78'⁰

75'⁴

Lanai

Stor.

Bedroom
12'⁴ • 11'¹⁰

Family Room
17'⁸ • 15'⁶

Bath

Breakfast
12'⁴ • 9'¹⁰

Lanai

Sitting

Bedroom
11'¹⁰ • 12'¹

w.i.c.

Living
14'² • 13'⁷

Bath

Master Bedroom
15'⁶ • 14'⁰

Utility

Kitchen
15'⁵ • 13'²

3 Car Garage
20'⁰ • 31'⁰

Dining
12'⁶ • 14'³

Foyer

Study
10'¹⁰ • 12'³

Master Bath

Entry

w.i.c.

One-Of-A-Kind Facade

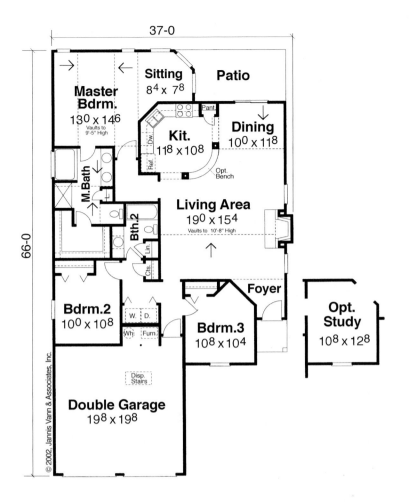

Total Square Feet - 1,532

Bedrooms - 3

Baths - 2

Garage - 2-car

Foundation - Basement or slab, please specify when ordering

Loaded with flexibility and lots of function, the kitchen design of this home includes an option for a curved bench creating more space for dining if needed. Enter the master bedroom and find a private bath with a walk-in closet and a sunny sitting area overlooking the outdoor patio perfect for quiet mornings or casual evenings. Plus, a practical bedroom #3 can easily be converted to a study with an additional entrance near the foyer. Whatever needs have to be met, this home provides the complete package.

Price Code B

A Home With A Custom Feel

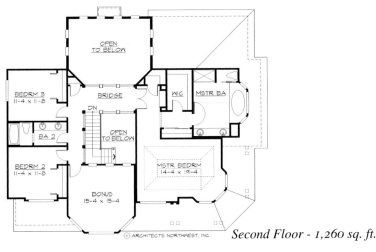

OPEN TO BELOW

BEDRM 3
11-4 x 11-8

BRIDGE

DN

WIC

MSTR BA

BA 2

OPEN TO BELOW

BEDRM 2
11-4 x 11-8

BONUS
15-4 x 15-4

MSTR BEDRM
14-4 x 19-4

© ARCHITECTS NORTHWEST, INC.

Second Floor - 1,260 sq. ft.

59'-0"

© ARCHITECTS NORTHWEST, INC.

PATIO

FAMILY
15-2 x 19-0

NOOK
9-8 x 14-2

UTIL

3-CAR GARAGE
22-4 x 29-4

KITCHEN
11-8 x 15-4

PDR

50'-0"

UP

FOYER

DEN
12-4 x 12-4

DINING
11-4 x 11-4

LIVING
15-4 x 15-4

COV'D PORCH

First Floor - 1,630 sq. ft.

Plan #587-071D-0003

Total Square Feet - 2,890

Bedrooms - 3

Baths - 2 1/2

Garage - 3-car side entry

Foundation - Crawl space

Formal dining and living rooms in the front of the home create a private place for entertaining. While a more casual area like the kitchen is designed for efficiency including a large island with cooktop and extra counterspace in route to the dining room. Extras can be found throughout the home, including the stunning oversized whirlpool tub showcased in the private master bath. Plus, the second floor bonus room has an additional 240 square feet of living area perfect for a private retreat or play area.

Price Code E

Victorian Style

6

Second Floor - 736 sq. ft.

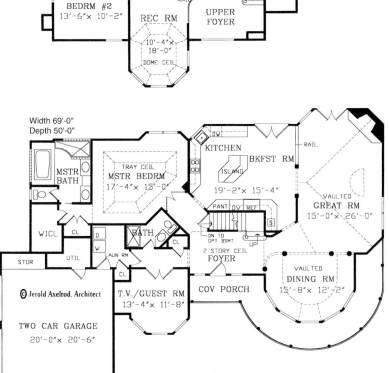

Plan #587-016D-0045

Total Square Feet - 2,696

Bedrooms - 4
Baths - 2 1/2
Garage - 2-car side entry

Foundation - Basement, crawl space
or slab, please specify when ordering

Turn-of-the-century style and
details can be found throughout this
beautiful home including a great
room featuring a corner design
fireplace. Plus, the dining room has
a 14' ceiling and beautiful sweeping
views onto the curved front porch
creating a sense of style from by-
gone years. The second floor is filled
with character as well, including
a turreted recreation room, two
bedrooms and a full bath all
perfectly designed for
comfortable family living.

Price Code F

First Floor - 1,960 sq. ft.

Courtyard Offers Landscaping Opportunities

Width: 71'-10"
Depth: 66'-10"

Deck
31'x 10'

Porch
18'2"x 10'

Breakfast
11'10"x 11'

Ma.
Bath

Master
Bedroom
14'6"x 18'4"

Walk-In
Closet

Bath

Living
22'x 17'

Kitchen
11'10"x 12'

Utility

WIC

Bedroom
11'8"x 12'6"

Foyer

Dining
13'8"x 12'

Pantry

1/2
Bath

Bedroom
11'4"x 13'

Porch

Three-Car
Garage
21'2"x 34'8"

Courtyard

Total Square Feet - 2,240
Bedrooms - 3
Baths - 2 1/2
Garage - 3-car side entry

*Foundation - Crawl space
or basement, please specify
when ordering*

*Designed to have social and private
areas, this home features all four
bedrooms on the left side maintaining
privacy from the more active living
areas. Certain to be a gathering
place, the breakfast area is bright
and cheery with an abundance of
windows making it the perfect way to
begin your day. Or, access the porch
and deck from the master bedroom
and living area for convenient
outdoor relaxation.*

Price Code H

High Style Dominates Living Spaces

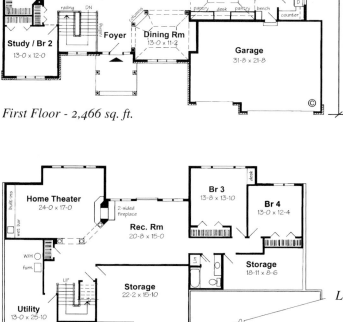

First Floor - 2,466 sq. ft.

Lower Level - 1,598 sq. ft.

Total Square Feet - 4,064

Bedrooms - 4

Baths - 3

Garage - 3-car

Foundation - Basement

Sleek lines add a contemporary feel to the front of this home. Meanwhile, the three-sided fireplace creates a cozy feeling to the kitchen, breakfast and hearth rooms. Decorative columns grace the corner of the formal dining room and help maintain an open feeling that resonates throughout this entire home due to the large open areas that are found on both the first floor and the lower level.

Price Code G

Stylish Features Throughout

First Floor - 3,171 sq. ft.

Total Square Feet - 3,171

Bedrooms - 3
Baths - 2 1/2
Garage - 3-car side entry
Foundation - Walk-out basement

The great room, breakfast area and kitchen combine with 12' ceilings to create an open feel throughout the interior. Organization is the key to the design in the master bath which contains an enormous walk-in closet and dressing area. The optional lower level has an additional 1,897 square feet of living area and is designed for entertaining featuring a wet bar with seating, a billiards room, large media room, two bedrooms and a full bath. Appealing amenities make this a magnificent plan.

Price Code E

Optional Lower Level - 1,897 sq. ft.

Spacious Country Charmer

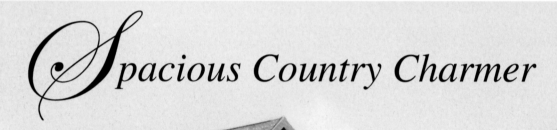

Second Floor - 728 sq. ft.

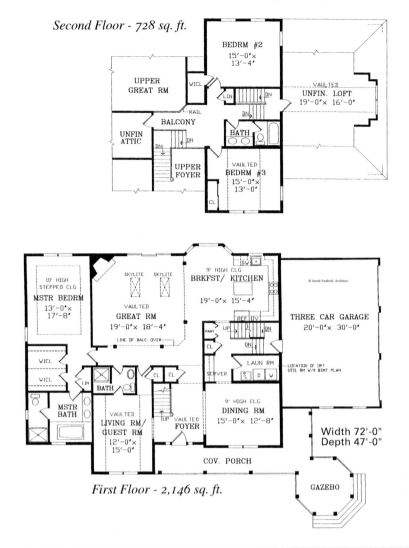

Plan #587-016D-0058

Total Square Feet - 2,874

Bedrooms - 4

Baths - 3

Garage - 3-car side entry

Foundation - Basement, crawl space
or slab, please specify when ordering

Openness characterizes the casual
areas in this home. The kitchen is
separated from the bayed breakfast
nook only by an island workspace
creating an overall spacious
atmosphere. The stunning great
room has a dramatic vaulted ceiling
and a corner fireplace adding to the
open feeling. Plus, the second floor
unfinished loft has an additional 300
square feet of living area perfect for
casual relaxation away from the main
living areas of the home.

Price Code G

First Floor - 2,146 sq. ft.

Width 72'-0"
Depth 47'-0"

Rich Details

Plan #587-051D-0186

Total Square Feet - 3,489
Bedrooms - 4
Baths - 3 1/2
Garage - 3-car side entry
Foundation - Basement

Two-story ceilings enhance the entry and great room greeting guests with a lovely, spacious atmosphere. In addition, an appealing nook is flooded with sunlight from the large windows and skylights above, also offering a bright, open environment. True function is achieved with the placement of a stovetop island and walk-in pantry in the large kitchen adding convenience and terrific organization to the most popular area of the home.

Price Code G

Second Floor - 975 sq. ft.

First Floor - 2,514 sq. ft.

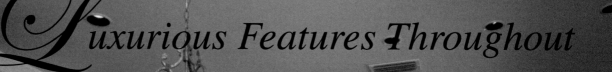

Plan #587-024D-0060

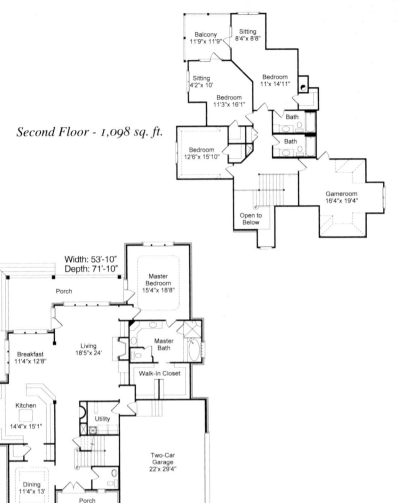

Second Floor - 1,098 sq. ft.

Second Floor rooms:
- Balcony 11'9"x 11'9"
- Sitting 8'4"x 8'8"
- Sitting 4'2"x 10'
- Bedroom 11'x 14'11"
- Bedroom 11'3"x 16'1"
- Bath
- Bath
- Bedroom 12'6"x 15'10"
- Gameroom 16'4"x 19'4"
- Open to Below

First Floor rooms:
- Width: 53'-10"
- Depth: 71'-10"
- Porch
- Master Bedroom 15'4"x 18'8"
- Breakfast 11'4"x 12'8"
- Living 18'5"x 24'
- Master Bath
- Walk-In Closet
- Kitchen 14'4"x 15'1"
- Utility
- Two-Car Garage 22'x 29'4"
- Dining 11'4"x 13'
- Porch

First Floor - 2,170 sq. ft.

Total Square Feet - 3,268

Bedrooms - 4

Baths - 3 1/2

Garage - 2-car side entry

Foundation - Slab

Stucco and brick combine to create a beautiful facade. As you enter the home, a grand entrance greets you with an elegant staircase and formal dining room just begging to be used for entertaining and family gatherings. Furthermore, the second floor includes three bedrooms, two of which open to the balcony and include their own sitting areas. Also, a future gameroom has an additional 323 square feet of living space offering even more possibilities for optimizing this home for a growing family's needs.

Price Code H

Luxury Home Filled With Extras Has A Custom Feel

Plan #587-047D-0056

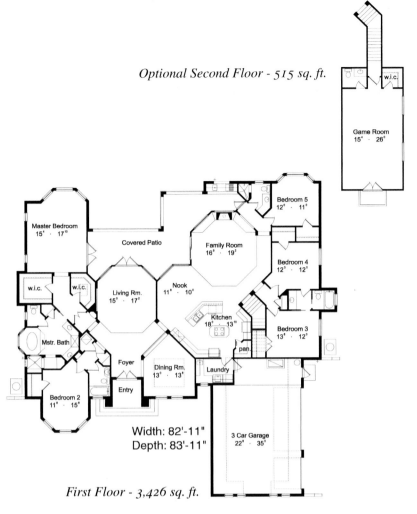

Optional Second Floor - 515 sq. ft.

Game Room
15⁴ · 26⁰

Master Bedroom
15⁴ · 17¹⁰

Covered Patio

Bedroom 5
12⁵ · 11⁵

Family Room
16⁰ · 19²

w.i.c.

w.i.c.

Living Rm.
15⁰ · 17²

Nook
11⁸ · 10⁰

Bedroom 4
12⁵ · 12⁵

Kitchen
18⁰ · 13¹⁰

Mstr. Bath

Bedroom 3
13⁵ · 12⁵

pan.

Foyer

Dining Rm.
13⁵ · 13⁵

Laundry

Bedroom 2
11⁴ · 15⁵

Entry

Width: 82'-11"
Depth: 83'-11"

3 Car Garage
22⁵ · 35⁵

First Floor - 3,426 sq. ft.

Total Square Feet - 3,426
Bedrooms - 5
Baths - 4
Garage - 3-car side entry
Foundation - Slab

Angled walls throughout add interest to every room especially the added ceiling and window treatments creating a custom feel to the plan. Open and airy, the kitchen looks into a cozy breakfast nook as well as the casual family room and beyond to the gracious covered patio with an outdoor kitchen perfect for year-round alfresco dining. Another beautiful amenity is the enormous master bath featuring double walk-in closets and a whirlpool tub under a bay window. This home pampers all those who reside here while offering even more tremendous space in a 515 square foot future space on the second floor.

Price Code F

Country Cottage For A Narrow Lot

Plan #587-055D-0350

Total Square Feet - 1,451

Bedrooms - 3

Baths - 2

Foundation - Slab or crawl space, please specify when ordering

A large covered front porch encourages outdoor relaxation and includes French doors that lead into the den where a cozy atmosphere is achieved. To the rear of the home the kitchen, dining area and grilling porch join together to form an exceptional gathering space. Travel to the second floor upstairs to view two secondary bedrooms with dormers that share a full bath.

Price Code B

First Floor - 868 sq. ft.

An Impressive Showplace

First Floor - 2,582 sq. ft.

Deck

Kitchen
15'1" x 18'7"

Breakfast
13'8" x 13'8"

Great Room
15'8" x 21'51

Master
Bedroom
14'4" x 19'11"

walk in closet

pantry

Laun.   Hall   Bath

Gallery

Dressing

Three-car Garage
22'2" x 29'8"

Dining Room
16'2" x 14'2"

Foyer

Porch

Library
11'8" x 12'7"

64'

70'8"

Total Square Feet - 4,328
Bedrooms - 3
Baths - 3 1/2
Garage - 3-car side entry
Foundation - Basement

Lower Level - 1,746 sq. ft.

Patio

Media Room
17'10" x 21'6"

Bedroom
14'1" x 12'9"

Bath

Basement

Bedroom
10'9" x 14'10"

Bath

Billiard Room
15'8" x 16'8"

Exercise
Room
10'11" x 10'10"

Basement

The extra-large gourmet kitchen and breakfast room offer a spacious area for chores and family gatherings, while providing a striking view through the great room to the fireplace wall. For convenience a butler's pantry is located in the hall leading to the dining room making planning a meal even easier especially when clearing and serving. An extravagant master bedroom and library round out the first floor. The home also includes a lavish lower level containing a media room, billiard room, exercise room and two additional bedrooms.

Price Code G

*I*deal Vacation Style For Views

Second Floor - 528 sq. ft.

Plan #587-024D-0008

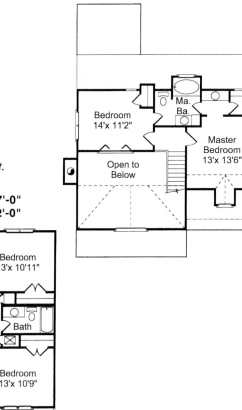

Total Square Feet - 1,650
Bedrooms - 4
Baths - 2
Foundation - Pier

First Floor - 1,122 sq. ft.

Width: 37'-0"
Depth: 52'-0"

The two-story living area features lots of windows for views to the outdoors and of the large fireplace from several places throughout the first floor. The open living area connects to the dining area in an effortless way while an adjacent kitchen is designed for efficiency and maintains an organized feel with a large island. A luxurious master bedroom is located on the second floor for privacy and enjoys its own private bath with an oversized whirlpool tub.

Price Code B

Dramatic Two-Story With
Half-Round Windows

Plan #587-016D-0046

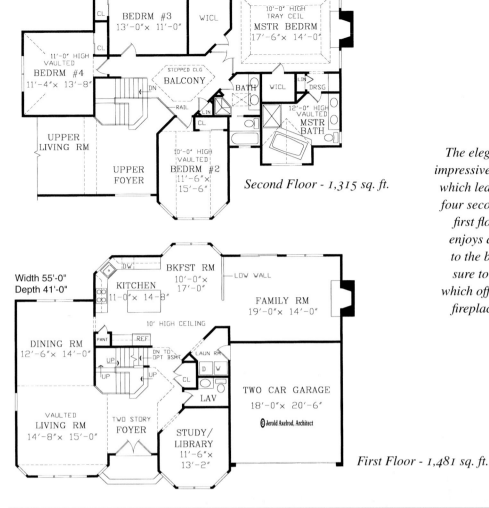

BEDRM #3
13'-0" × 11'-0"

WICL

10'-0" HIGH TRAY CEIL
MSTR BEDRM
17'-6" × 14'-0"

CL

11'-0" HIGH VAULTED
BEDRM #4
11'-4" × 13'-8"

STEPPED CLG
BALCONY

DN

RAIL

BATH

WICL

LIN

DRSG

CL

12'-0" HIGH VAULTED
MSTR BATH

LIN

CL

UPPER LIVING RM

UPPER FOYER

10'-0" HIGH VAULTED
BEDRM #2
11'-6" × 15'-6"

Second Floor - 1,315 sq. ft.

Width 55'-0"
Depth 41'-0"

DW

BKFST RM
10'-0" × 17'-0"

— LOW WALL

KITCHEN
11'-0" × 14'-8"

FAMILY RM
19'-0" × 14'-0"

10' HIGH CEILING

PANT

REF

DINING RM
12'-6" × 14'-0"

UP

DN TO OPT BSMT

LAUN RM

UP

D W

UP

CL

TWO CAR GARAGE
18'-0" × 20'-6"

LAV

© Jerold Axelrod, Architect

VAULTED
LIVING RM
14'-8" × 15'-0"

TWO STORY FOYER

STUDY/ LIBRARY
11'-6" × 13'-2"

First Floor - 1,481 sq. ft.

Total Square Feet - 2,796

Bedrooms - 4

Baths - 2 1/2

Garage - 2-car

Foundation - Basement

The elegant two-story foyer has an impressive view of the open stairway which leads to a railed balcony and four second floor bedrooms. On the first floor a spacious family room enjoys a fireplace and glass doors to the backyard. Homeowners are sure to enjoy the master bedroom which offers a 10' tray ceiling, cozy fireplace and two walk-in closets.

Price Code F

Stylish And Sophisticated

Second Floor - 1,071 sq. ft.

coffered clg.

Great Room Below

Balcony

Br 2
15-10x12-0

Br 3
12-0x13-6

Dn

open to below

Br 4
12-8x12-8

Plan #587-007D-0132

Total Square Feet - 4,370
Bedrooms - 4
Baths - 3 1/2
Garage - 3-car side entry
Foundation - Walk-out basement

Detailed brickwork surrounding the arched windows and quoined corners create a timeless exterior. The two-story great room boasts a large fireplace, flanking bookshelves, a massive window wall and balcony overlook. A state-of-the-art kitchen is sure to please any chef and offers an island cooktop, built-in oven/ microwave oven, large pantry, menu desk and opens to the breakfast and hearth rooms. A coffered ceiling, bay window, two walk-in closets and a huge bath adorn the master bedroom.

Price Code G

81'-8"

Deck

coffered clg.

MBr
20-0x16-6

Great Room
19-1x23-10

Brk Rm
15-0x12-9

Hearth Rm
16-0x14-0

Kit
15-0x14-4

Desk

L R

Dn
Up

Entry

Dining
12-0x14-4
tray clg.

P

Laundry
W D

Parlor
18-0x13-8
vaulted

Covered Porch

Garage
22-4x32-0

72'-6"

First Floor - 3,299 sq. ft.

Grand Features Throughout

Second Floor - 636 sq. ft.

Width: 40'-6"
Depth: 40'-0"

First Floor - 1,244 sq. ft.

Total Square Feet - 1,880

Bedrooms - 3
Baths - 2 1/2
Foundation - Crawl space

The large front porch welcomes guests into the home and is a perfect spot to sit back and relax. The first floor bedroom includes a private bath with double-bowl vanity and a walk-in closet, creating an ideal master suite. The secondary bedrooms enjoy walk-in closets and share a Jack and Jill bath.

Price Code C

Delightful Kitchen Adds Charm

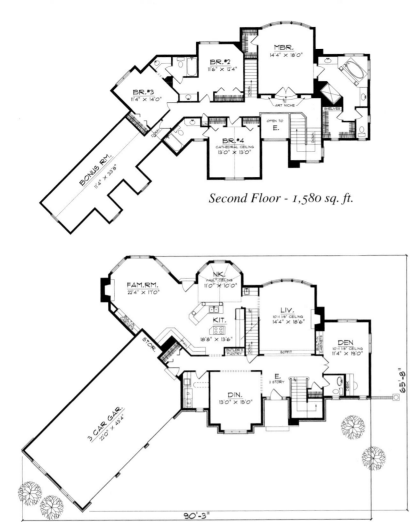

Second Floor - 1,580 sq. ft.

Total Square Feet - 3,511

Bedrooms - 4

Baths - 3 1/2

Garage - 3-car side entry

Foundation - Basement

The two-story entry leads into the grand living room which features a bowed window and cozy fireplace. The bayed nook and family room combine with the kitchen to create a relaxing area. All bedrooms are located on the second floor for additional privacy. The second floor also includes a bonus room which provides an additional 440 square feet of living area.

Price Code G

First Floor - 1,931 sq. ft.

Luxury Galore

56

Second Floor - 2,272 sq. ft.

Total Square Feet - 5,548

Bedrooms - 5
Baths - 4 1/2
Garage - 3-car side entry

Foundation - Basement, crawl space
or slab, please specify when ordering

The kitchen, breakfast and hearth rooms combine creating a natural gathering place. Many extras are featured throughout the design including a corner computer room off the kitchen and a hobby/exercise room. The nearby laundry room has plenty of space to make the household chore a breeze. The master bedroom is a glorious retreat and enjoys a vaulted bath. Four spacious secondary bedrooms and a large game room/home theater complete this grand home.

Price Code H

First Floor - 3,276 sq. ft.

French Country Delight

Second Floor - 1,091 sq. ft.

Plan #587-065D-0043

Total Square Feet - 3,816

Bedrooms - 4

Baths - 3 1/2

Garage - 3-car side entry

Foundation - Basement

An elegant library can be found off the foyer and is adjoined by the beautifully designed master bedroom with a lavish dressing area. The two-story great room has an impressive arched opening and a beautiful beamed ceiling. Nearby, the hearth room is a cozy place to relax and accesses the outdoor covered deck with a popular fireplace. The second floor computer loft is centrally located and includes plenty of counterspace, rounding out this wonderful family home.

Price Code F

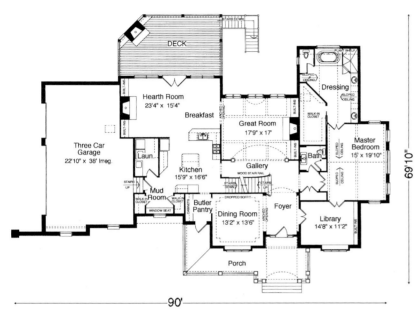

First Floor - 2,725 sq. ft.

Gorgeous Award-Winning Victorian

Plan #587-071D-0010

Second Floor - 2,875 sq. ft.

Total Square Feet - 5,250
Bedrooms - 4
Baths - 4 1/2
Garage - 4-car side entry
Foundation - Crawl space

The spacious wrap-around covered porch features an outdoor fireplace and built-in barbecue grill perfect for entertaining. Inside, the dramatic circular staircase is highlighted in a rotunda with a 27' ceiling. Each bedroom is pure luxury and enjoys its own bath and walk-in closet, with the master bath featuring an octagon-shaped space with a whirlpool tub. This home is truly amazing.

Price Code H

First Floor - 2,375 sq. ft.

71'-0"

91'-6"

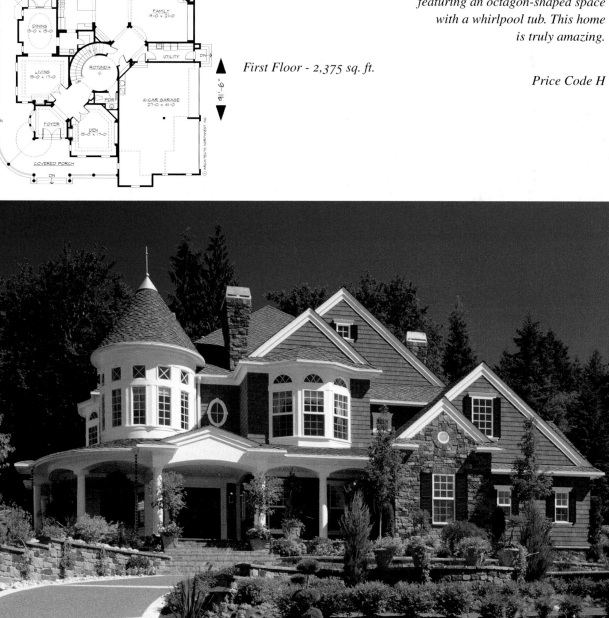

Inviting Family Home

Porch
22'11"x 10'5"

Master
Bedroom
15'x 19'6"

Master
Bath

Walk-In
Closet

Breakfast
13'6"x 12'6"

Living
20'11"x 17'

Bath

Bedroom
12'8"x 11'2"

Hall

Kitchen
11'x 14'

w
d

Dining
13'x 13'

Foyer

Bedroom
12'6"x 11'6"

Bedroom
12'8"x 11'

Utility

Porch

Two-Car
Garage
21'2"x 21'8"

Width: 62'-10"
Depth: 74'-3"

Total Square Feet - 2,471

Bedrooms - 4
Baths - 2 1/2
Garage - 2-car side entry

Foundation - Slab

Upon entering the home your eyes will catch the decorative columns that define the formal dining room. The adjoining living room is spacious and enjoys a warm fireplace and porch access. The kitchen and breakfast area combine and maintain openness with the living room. The right side of the home is for relaxing with all the bedrooms situated together.

Price Code E

Second Floor - 1,285 sq. ft.

Plant Shelf Above

Sitting
8^6 x 10^0

Bdrm. 3
11^0 x 11^6

M. Bdrm.
16^6 x 13^6

Tray Ceiling

Computer Station

Bath 2

M. Bath

Plant Shelf Above

Plant Shelf Above

Bdrm. 2
13^0 x 12^4

Desk

Bath 3

Bdrm. 4 w/ Office
14^2 x 16^6

Optional Built-in Bunk Beds

Total Square Feet - 3,011
Bedrooms - 4
Baths - 3 1/2
Garage - 2-car

Foundation - Walk-out basement

This uniquely designed home is filled with charm and is sure to delight all who enter. The spacious kitchen features an extra-large island, walk-in pantry and connects to the enormous family room. Nearby, a large laundry room provides enough space to make the household chores a breeze. All the bedrooms are located on the second floor and include plenty of built-ins for added convenience.

Price Code F

Patio

Width: 44'-0"
Depth: 62'-0"

Dw.

Pantry

Family
21^8 x 17^6

Beams

Shelves

Shelves

Hinged Seat w/ Ct Hooks Above

Cubby's

Kitchen
13^2 x 21^6

Lnd.

Ref.

W. D.

Up

Dn

Foyer
6^0 x 9^6

Butler's Pantry

C.

Lav. **Storage**

Dining
15^6 x 11^0

Double Garage
21^8 x 21^4

Front Porch

First Floor - 1,726 sq. ft.

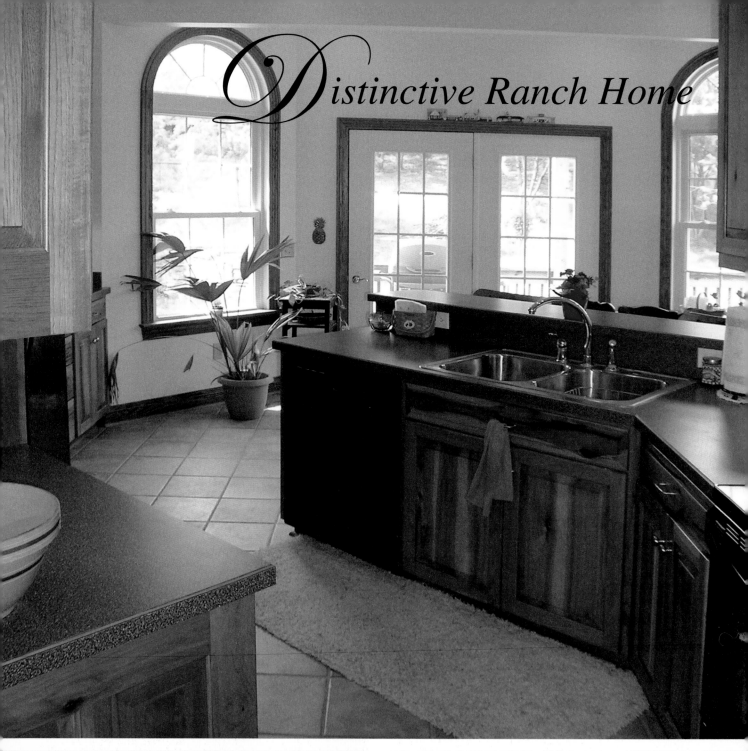

Distinctive Ranch Home

Plan #587-016D-0047

Total Square Feet - 1,860
Bedrooms - 3
Baths - 2
Garage - 2-car side entry

Foundation - Basement, crawl space
or slab, please specify when ordering

*The foyer opens to the formal dining
room which features an 11' stepped
ceiling and bay window creating
an elegant dining atmosphere. The
breakfast room has a 12' sloped
ceiling with French doors leading to
a covered porch and is the perfect
place to start your day. Continuing
the elegance, the great room has a
columned arched entrance, built-in
media center and fireplace.*

Price Code D

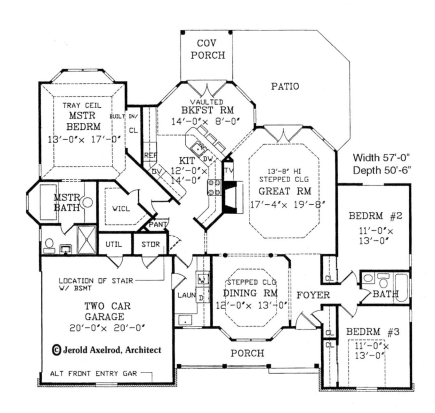

COV
PORCH

PATIO

VAULTED
BKFST RM
14'-0" x 8'-0"

TRAY CEIL
MSTR
BEDRM
13'-0" x 17'-0"

BUILT IN/
CL

REF

KIT
12'-0" x
14'-0"

DW

DV

TV

13'-8" HI
STEPPED CLG
GREAT RM
17'-4" x 19'-8"

Width 57'-0"
Depth 50'-6"

MSTR
BATH

WICL

PANT

BEDRM #2
11'-0" x
13'-0"

UTIL

STOR

LOCATION OF STAIR
W/ BSMT

LAUN

W
D

STEPPED CLG
DINING RM
12'-0" x 13'-0"

FOYER

CL

BATH

CL

TWO CAR
GARAGE
20'-0" x 20'-0"

© Jerold Axelrod, Architect

PORCH

BEDRM #3
11'-0" x
13'-0"

CL

ALT FRONT ENTRY GAR

Arched Windows Add Style

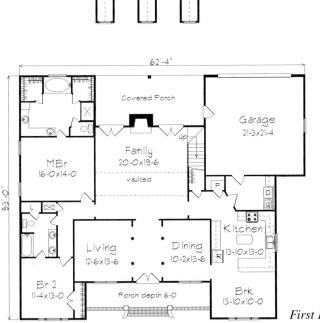

Second Floor - 717 sq. ft.

open to below

Loft

Balcony

Dn

Br 4
11-0x11-6

Br 3
11-0x11-6

L

Total Square Feet - 2,869

Bedrooms - 4

Baths - 3

Garage - 2-car rear entry

Foundation - Slab, drawings also
include crawl space

*The Traditional-style foyer is flanked
by columned living and dining rooms
and leads to the vaulted family room
with a fireplace and twin sets of
French doors. With the main living
areas centralized, the bedrooms
find it easy to become spaces for
pure relaxation. High ceilings add
to the spaciousness of the plan with
10' ceilings on the first floor and 9'
ceilings on the second floor.*

Price Code E

62'-4"

Covered Porch

Garage
21-3x21-4

Family
20-0x19-6

vaulted

MBr
16-0x14-0

53'-0"

up

P

L

D

Kitchen
13-10x13-0

Living
12-6x13-6

Dining
10-2x13-6

R

Br 2
11-4x13-0

Porch depth 6-0

Brk
13-10x10-0

First Floor - 2,152 sq. ft.

Elegant Touches Grace Home

Second Floor - 936 sq. ft.

Total Square Feet - 3,291

Bedrooms - 4

Baths - 3 1/2

Garage - 4-car side entry

Foundation - Basement

The two-story family room boasts a grand fireplace flanked by built-in shelves. Nearby, the kitchen and bayed nook connect with the sunroom which creates a warm and cheerful atmosphere. On the opposite side of the home, the elegant master bedroom features a bayed sitting area and double-door entry to the deluxe bath with vaulted ceiling. The secondary bedrooms comprise the second floor and enjoy walk-in closets.

Price Code G

First Floor - 2,355 sq. ft.

Stunning Details

Plan #587-052D-0121

Second Floor - 1,835 sq. ft.

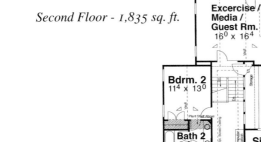

Bath 3

Excercise /
Media /
Guest Rm.
16^0 x 16^4

Bdrm. 2
11^4 x 13^0

Bath 2

Sitting
11^4 x 8^8

Bdrm. 3
10^6 x 12^6

Master Bdrm.
17^6 x 17^8

M.Closet

M. Bath

Total Square Feet - 3,223

Bedrooms - 4

Baths - 3 1/2

Garage - 2-car rear entry

Foundation - Basement

Upon entering the home you will view the stunning living room with grand fireplace and decorative ceiling. Adjoining this wonderful space is the kitchen, breakfast and keeping rooms that create an open environment for an easy flow of family activities. The living and keeping rooms access the screen porch which is ideal for outdoor living. All the bedrooms are located on the second floor and enjoy use of the exercise/media/game room. A built-in computer station nearby is the perfect place for children to do schoolwork.

Price Code F

Double Garage
21^4 x 21^4

Lnd.
11^4 x 9^0

Patio

Brkfst.
11^8 x 11^8

Keeping
12^0 x 14^8

Screen
Porch

Kitchen
15^6 x 15^2

Living
17^6 x 17^4

Dining
15^6 x 11^6

Foyer

Lav.

Pantry

First Floor - 1,388 sq. ft.

Width: 37'-6"
Depth: 70'-0"

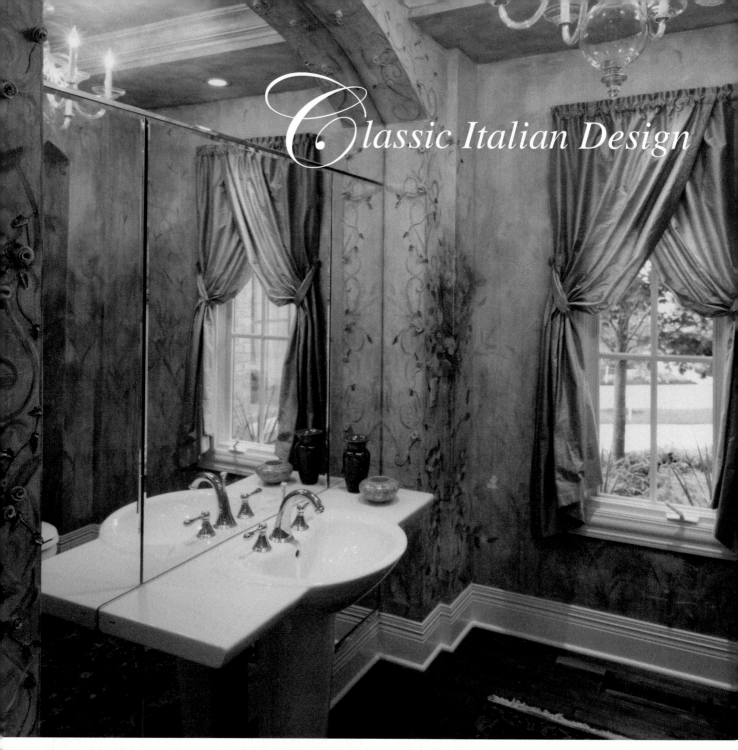

Classic Italian Design

Second Floor - 1,820 sq. ft.

Bedroom
18'1" x 17'6"
9' CEILING HEIGHT

Bath

Open to Below

Gallery
9' CEILING HEIGHT

Balcony

WALK-IN CLOSET

WALK-IN CLOSET

DROPPED SOFFIT

WALK-IN CLOSET

Bedroom
14' x 17'10"
9' CEILING HEIGHT

Bath

Bedroom
14' x 17'10"
9' CEILING HEIGHT

Dressing
9' CEILING HEIGHT

Court Yard
Below

Total Square Feet - 5,143

Bedrooms - 4

Baths - 3 1/2

Garage - 3-car side entry

Foundation - Walk-out basement

The first floor has an enormous amount of luxury including a grand foyer and library both with custom cabinetry, and an impressive master bedroom with lavish dressing area and walk-in closet. The second floor bedrooms all have walk-in closets and 9' ceilings while enjoying the hall gallery. The optional lower level offers an additional 1,351 square feet of living area and includes a sitting room with fireplace, media center, wine storage and an exercise room. Every inch of this home is stunning.

Price Code H

Master
Bedroom
17'8" X 17'

Great Room
17'9" x 29'4"
CEILING HEIGHT 18'4"

Deck

Kitchen
16'9" x 19'6"

Laun.

Dressing

STAIRS UP

Dining

Pantry

Three Car
Garage
23'6" x 37'2"

Hakka

CUSTOM CABINETS

Mud
Room

WALK-IN CLOSET

DRAWER BASE

Library
14' X 16'4"

CEILING HEIGHT 18'4"

Foyer
17'9" x 11'4"

Dining
Room
14' x 16'4"

Bath

WALK-IN CLOSET

Court Yard

60'6"

First Floor - 3,323 sq. ft.

113'10"

Deluxe Living Areas

Second Floor - 716 sq. ft.

First Floor - 3,185 sq. ft.

Total Square Feet - 3,901

Bedrooms - 3

Baths - 4

Garage - 2-car side entry

Foundation - Slab or crawl space, please specify when ordering

An elegant foyer opens into the column-lined dining room for a formal atmosphere. Nearby, the spacious kitchen will please any chef and features an island bar with seating. The exquisite master suite offers a boxed ceiling, sitting room and private bath with whirlpool tub flanked by columns. A nursery/office nearby makes this home ideal for many life stages.

Price Code G

Stately Living In A Family Home

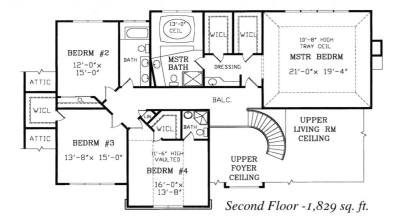

BEDRM #2
12'-0"×
15'-0"

ATTIC

WICL

CL

ATTIC

BATH

MSTR BATH

13'-0" CEIL

WICL WICL

DRESSING

MSTR BEDRM
21'-0" × 19'-4"

10'-8" HIGH TRAY CEIL

BALC.

LIN

WICL BATH

BEDRM #3
13'-8" × 15'-0"

11'-6" HIGH VAULTED

BEDRM #4
16'-0" × 13'-8"

UPPER FOYER CEILING

UPPER LIVING RM CEILING

Second Floor -1,829 sq. ft.

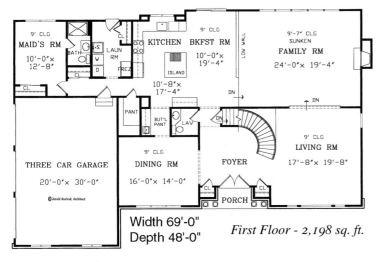

9' CLG
MAID'S RM
10'-0"×
12'-8"

BATH

LAUN RM

FREZ

CL

KITCHEN

ISLAND

10'-8"×
17'-4"

BKFST RM
10'-0"×
19'-4"

9' CLG

LOV WALL

9'-7" CLG
SUNKEN
FAMILY RM
24'-0"× 19'-4"

CL

PANT

BUT'L PANT

LAV

DN

DN

DN

THREE CAR GARAGE
20'-0"× 30'-0"

Jerold Axelrod, Architect

9' CLG
DINING RM
16'-0"× 14'-0"

FOYER

9' CLG
LIVING RM
17'-8"× 19'-8"

CL

CL

PORCH

Width 69'-0"
Depth 48'-0"

First Floor - 2,198 sq. ft.

Total Square Feet - 4,027

Bedrooms - 5

Baths - 4 1/2

Garage - 3-car side entry

Foundation - Basement or crawl space, please specify when ordering

The foyer offers an impressive view of the grand staircase and opens into the formal living and dining rooms. The sunken family room provides a cozy atmosphere while remaining open to the kitchen and breakfast room. The pampering master bedroom includes a dressing area, two walk-in closets and a radiant bath.

Price Code H

Historical Architecture

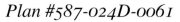

Second Floor - 1,206 sq. ft.

Bedroom #2
13'x 15'6"

WIC

Ba.

Unfinished
Area

Balcony

Unfinished
Area

WIC

WIC

Bath

Bedroom #3
13'6"x 14'

Open to
Below

Bedroom #4
13'6"x 12'2"

WIC

Width: 59'-4"
Depth: 64'-0"

Wood Deck
30'10"x 13'

Porch
30'5"x 8'

First Floor - 2,129 sq. ft.

Breakfast
11'4"x 13'

Living
21'6"x 17'2"

Master
Bedroom
16'4"x 16'4"

Util.

WIC

WIC

Kitchen
11'4"x 18'4"

Bath

WIC

Ma.
Bath

Porch

Dining
13'6"x 13'10"

Foyer

Study
13'8"x 12'

Porch

Porch
36'x 7'

Storage
16'x 8'

Gameroom
21'3"x 17'

Two Car
Garage
25'x 24'

Extra
Storage
12'9"x 10'

Optional Lower Level - 435 sq. ft.

Plan #587-024D-0061

Total Square Feet - 3,335

Bedrooms - 4

Baths - 4

Garage - 2-car drive under

Foundation - Basement

This home features the comfort of a country cottage with modern amenities providing convenience and luxury. The dining room and study have two sets of French doors brightening the area. The unfinished areas on the second floor have an additional 422 square feet of living space. The lower level gameroom is an ideal place for entertaining and has an additional 435 square feet of living space.

Price Code H

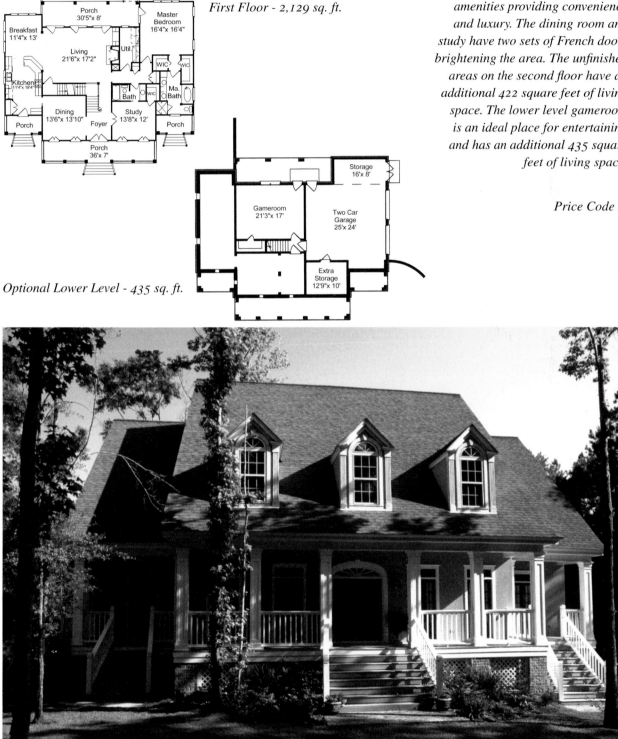

Exquisite Details Throughout

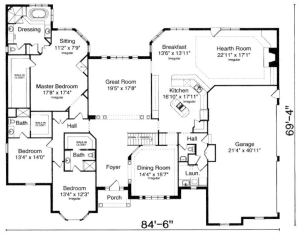

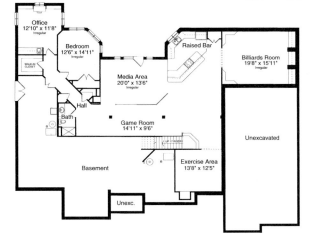

First Floor - 3,421 sq. ft.

Optional Lower Level - 1,777 sq. ft.

Plan #587-065D-0078

Total Square Feet - 3,421
Bedrooms - 3
Baths - 3 1/2
Garage - 4-car side entry
Foundation - Basement

This grand home is sure to please with elegant features throughout. The gourmet kitchen with island and snack bar combine with the spacious breakfast and hearth rooms to create a warm and friendly atmosphere. The luxurious master bedroom with sitting area and fireplace is complemented by a deluxe bath designed to pamper. The optional lower level has an additional 1,777 square feet of living area and offers fun and excitement.

Price Code F

Decorative Ceilings Grace Rooms

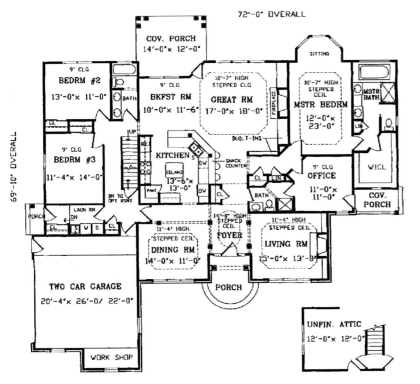

Total Square Feet - 2,585
Bedrooms - 3
Baths - 2 1/2
Garage - 2-car side entry

Foundation - Basement, slab or crawl space, please specify when ordering

An impressive foyer is flanked by the formal living and dining rooms which feature pillar framed entrances and stepped ceilings. The kitchen includes a walk-in pantry and angled serving counter for added convenience. A sensational master bedroom enjoys a bayed sitting area, huge walk-in closet and large private bath. Two secondary bedrooms on the opposite side round out this family home.

Price Code D

Grand Two-Story

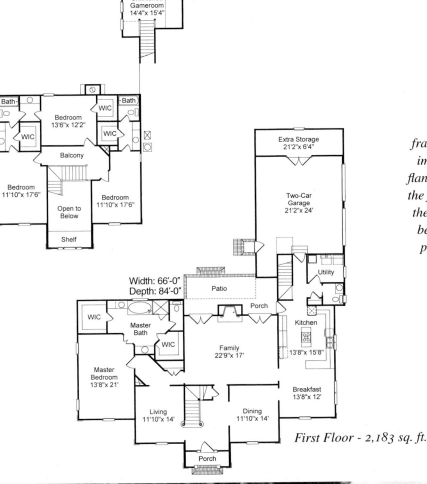

Second Floor - 993 sq. ft.

Unfinished
Gameroom
14'4"x 15'4"

Bath

Bath

WIC

WIC

WIC

Bedroom
13'6"x 12'2"

Bedroom
11'10"x 17'6"

Balcony

Bedroom
11'10"x 17'6"

Open to
Below

Shelf

Extra Storage
21'2"x 6'4"

Two-Car
Garage
21'2"x 24'

Utility

Width: 66'-0"
Depth: 84'-0"

Patio

Porch

WIC

Master
Bath

Kitchen
13'8"x 15'8"

WIC

Family
22'9"x 17'

Master
Bedroom
13'8"x 21'

Breakfast
13'8"x 12'

Living
11'10"x 14'

Dining
11'10"x 14'

Porch

First Floor - 2,183 sq. ft.

Plan #587-024D-0058

Total Square Feet - 3,176
Bedrooms - 4
Baths - 3 1/2
Garage - 2-car side entry
Foundation - Slab

Formal dining and living rooms frame the foyer for a Traditional, yet impressive feel. A grand fireplace is flanked by French doors leading from the family room to the rear porch. On the second floor, spacious secondary bedrooms enjoy walk-in closets and private bath access. The unfinished gameroom has an additional 255 square feet of living area.

Price Code G

Unique European Chalet

Second Floor - 1,075 sq. ft.

Total Square Feet - 3,650
Bedrooms - 4
Baths - 3 1/2
Garage - 4-car side entry
Foundation - Basement

A two-story vaulted ceiling enhances the spacious great room which features a grand fireplace flanked by built-ins. The expansive kitchen/nook area features a cooktop island with seating, walk-in pantry and access to the outdoors. Entertain with ease in the formal dining room with step ceiling and nearby butler's pantry. On the second floor, bedroom #4 provides a wonderful suite with a study area, walk-in closet and private bath.

Price Code G

First Floor - 2,575 sq. ft.

Splendid Great Room

Total Square Feet - 2,041
Bedrooms - 3
Baths - 2
Garage - 2-car side entry
Foundation - Walk-out basement

Beyond the elegant foyer is the spacious great room which accesses the covered rear deck with ceiling fan above. The private master bedroom enjoys a beautiful octagon-shaped sitting area that opens and brightens the space. On the opposite side of the home two secondary bedrooms share a full bath.

Price Code C

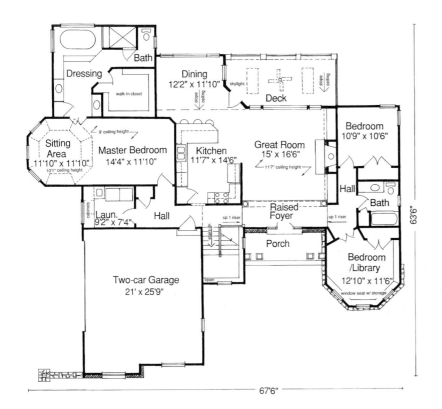

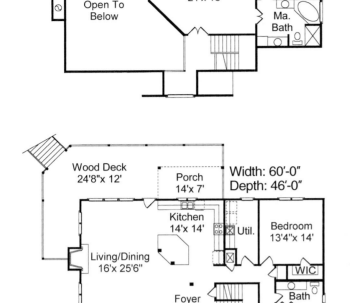

Balcony
14'x 7'

Second Floor - 653 sq. ft.

Open To
Below

Master
Bedroom
21'x 18'

WIC

Ma.
Bath

Total Square Feet - 2,205

Bedrooms - 3

Baths - 2

Garage - 2-car drive under carport

Foundation - Pier

The double-door entry opens to the spacious two-story living/dining area and kitchen with unique center island. Two secondary bedrooms are secluded from the living areas and enjoy walk-in closets and a shared bath. On the second floor, the private master bedroom enjoys a deluxe bath and balcony. Escape from all your stress in this relaxing retreat.

Price Code C

Wood Deck
24'8"x 12'

Porch
14'x 7'

Width: 60'-0"
Depth: 46'-0"

Kitchen
14'x 14'

Util.

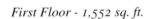

Bedroom
13'4"x 14'

Living/Dining
16'x 25'6"

WIC

Foyer

Bath

Porch
21'6"x 8'

Bedroom
13'4"x 11'4"

First Floor - 1,552 sq. ft.

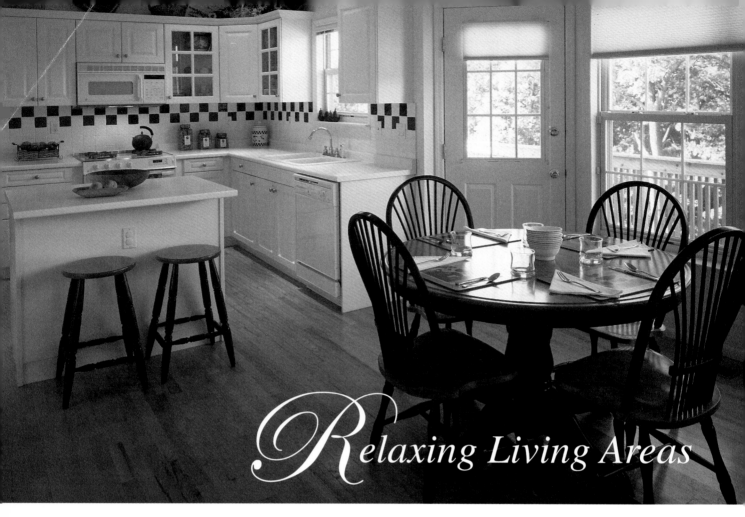

Relaxing Living Areas

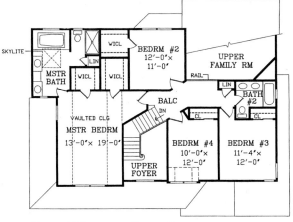

Second Floor - 1,180 sq. ft.

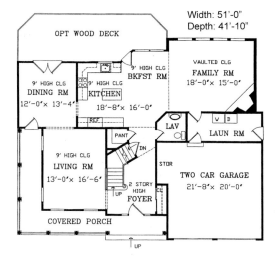

Width: 51'-0"
Depth: 41'-10"

First Floor - 1,290 sq. ft.

Total Square Feet - 2,470

Bedrooms - 4
Baths - 2 1/2
Garage - 2-car

Foundation - Basement, walk-out basement, crawl space or slab, please specify when ordering

A cheerful family area is created with the U-shaped kitchen opening into the breakfast and family rooms. Formal living and dining rooms add elegance and create an ideal place for entertaining. On the second floor, the vaulted master bedroom features two walk-in closets and a private bath, while three secondary bedrooms complete this functional family home.

Price Code F

$\mathcal{B}$right & Luxurious Home

Plan #587-051D-0182

Total Square Feet - 2,600
Bedrooms - 3
Baths - 2 1/2
Garage - 3-car side entry
Foundation - Basement

The entry of this gorgeous home opens into the spacious great room which features a wall of windows bringing in an abundance of light. The kitchen enjoys plenty of counterspace including an extra-large island. Step into the master bedroom which boasts a double-door entry, sitting area, two walk-in closets and a private bath. To complete the home, the convenient laundry area includes a closet, sink and an alternate stairway to the basement.

Price Code F

Design Dedicated To Comfort

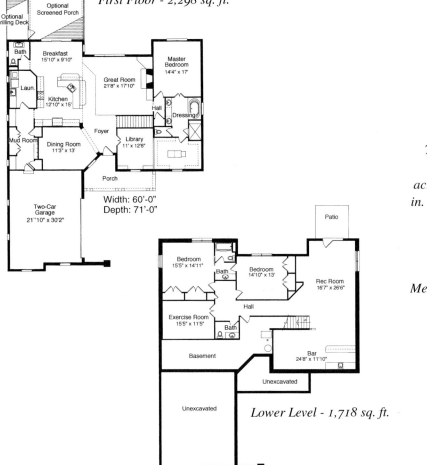

First Floor - 2,298 sq. ft.

Optional Grilling Deck

Optional Screened Porch

Bath

Breakfast
15'10" x 9'10"

Laun.

Kitchen
12'10" x 15'

Mud Room

Dining Room
11'3" x 13'

Foyer

Porch

Great Room
21'8" x 17'10"

Master Bedroom
14'4" x 17'

Hall

Dressing

Library
11' x 12'6"

Two-Car Garage
21'10" x 30'2"

Width: 60'-0"
Depth: 71'-0"

Patio

Bedroom
15'5" x 14'11"

Bath

Bedroom
14'10" x 13'

Rec Room
16'7" x 26'6"

Hall

Exercise Room
15'5" x 11'5"

Bath

Basement

Bar
24'8" x 11'10"

Unexcavated

Unexcavated

Lower Level - 1,718 sq. ft.

Plan #587-065D-0114

Total Square Feet - 4,016

Bedrooms - 3
Baths - 2 full, 2 half
Garage - 2-car side entry
Foundation - Walk-out basement

The great room is warmed by a gas fireplace and a wall of windows across the rear bringing the outdoors in. A wrap-around island with seating is adorned with arched openings and separates the kitchen from the great room and breakfast area in a beautiful and effortless way. Meanwhile dramatic triple doors lead to a delightful screened porch and adjacent grilling deck.

Price Code D

Elegant Outdoor Living

Second Floor - 1,398 sq. ft.

Plan #587-024D-0062

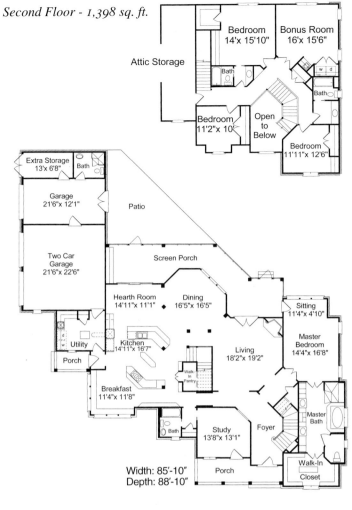

Attic Storage

Bedroom
14'x 15'10"

Bonus Room
16'x 15'6"

Bath

w d

Bath

Bedroom
11'2"x 10'

Open to Below

Bedroom
11'11"x 12'6"

Extra Storage
13'x 6'8"

Bath

Garage
21'6"x 12'1"

Patio

Two Car Garage
21'6"x 22'6"

Screen Porch

Hearth Room
14'11"x 11'1"

Dining
16'5"x 16'5"

Sitting
11'4"x 4'10"

Master Bedroom
14'4"x 16'8"

Utility

Porch

Kitchen
14'11"x 16'7"

Living
18'2"x 19'2"

Breakfast
11'4"x 11'8"

Walk-In Pantry

Bath

Study
13'8"x 13'1"

Foyer

Master Bath

Width: 85'-10"
Depth: 88'-10"

Porch

Walk-In Closet

First Floor - 2,859 sq. ft.

Total Square Feet - 4,257
Bedrooms - 4
Baths - 4 1/2
Garage - 3-car side entry
Foundation - Slab

Unique angles throughout this house add style to the interior. The living areas are open to each other with the dining area defined by decorative columns. The utility room doubles as a hobby room and includes a TV cabinet for plenty of flexibility and organization. Enjoy the master bedroom featuring a sitting area, exquisite bath and a large walk-in closet maintaining a neat appearance.

Price Code H

Exquisite European Design

First Floor - 2,055 sq. ft.

Lower Level - 1,854 sq. ft.

Plan #587-051D-0188

Total Square Feet - 3,909

Bedrooms - 4

Baths - 2 full, 2 half

Garage - 3-car side entry

Foundation - Walk-out basement

The spacious entry opens into the great room and offers a grand first impression with a 15' ceiling. Or, look inside the open kitchen and discover a massive pantry and snack bar island that is open to the formal dining room and cozy hearth room. Descend to the lower level and find three secondary bedrooms, a recreation room and entertaining area with wet bar.

Price Code G

Home Filled With Amenities

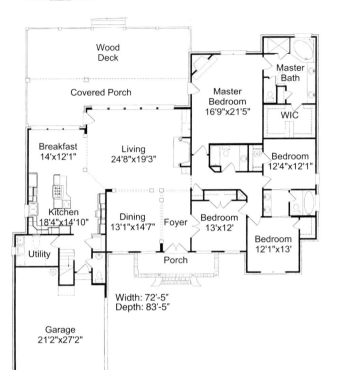

Optional Second Floor - 304 sq. ft.

Gameroom
13'5"x17'

Wood
Deck

Covered Porch

Breakfast
14'x12'1"

Living
24'8"x19'3"

Kitchen
18'4"x14'10"

Master
Bedroom
16'9"x21'5"

Master
Bath

WIC

Bedroom
12'4"x12'1"

Dining
13'1"x14'7"

Foyer

Bedroom
13'x12'

Bedroom
12'1"x13'

Utility

Porch

Width: 72'-5"
Depth: 83'-5"

Garage
21'2"x27'2"

First Floor - 2,968 sq. ft.

Total Square Feet - 2,968
Bedrooms - 4
Baths - 3 1/2
Garage - 2-car side entry
Foundation - Slab

*Decorative columns accent
the entrance and define the
formal dining room. Nearby, a
full wall of windows brightens the
living room which also enjoys an
inviting fireplace. Step inside the
spacious kitchen and find a space
designed for efficiency and open
to the splendid breakfast room
nearby. Plus, this home has an
optional second floor with
an additional 304 square feet
of living area perfect for
expansion when needed.*

Price Code H

Plan #587-013D-0022

Total Square Feet - 1,992

Bedrooms - 4

Baths - 3

Garage - 2-car side entry

Foundation - Basement, crawl space
or slab, please specify when ordering

Interesting angled walls add
drama to many of the living
areas including the family room,
master bedroom and breakfast area.
And, enjoy the outdoors with a
covered porch including a spa
and an outdoor kitchen with sink,
refrigerator and cooktop. Luxury
can also be found in the majestic
master bath where a dramatic corner
oversized tub resides in a secluded
atmosphere.

Price Code C

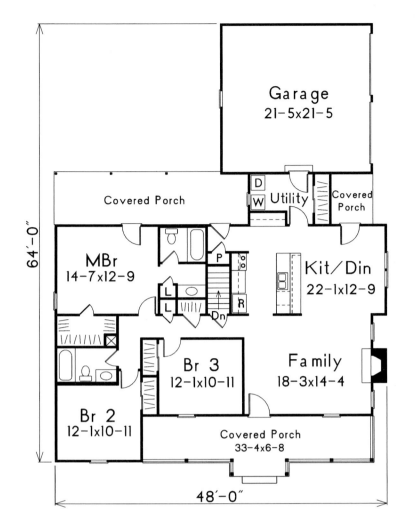

Plan #587-001D-0031

Garage
21-5x21-5

Covered Porch

D
W Utility

Covered Porch

MBr
14-7x12-9

P

Kit/Din
22-1x12-9

L
L
R
Dn

Br 3
12-1x10-11

Family
18-3x14-4

Br 2
12-1x10-11

Covered Porch
33-4x6-8

64'-0"

48'-0"

Total Square Feet - 1,501

Bedrooms - 3

Baths - 2

Garage - 2-car side entry

Foundation - Basement foundation, drawings also include crawl space and slab

The large family room creates an open feeling as soon as you enter this home. Add a spacious kitchen with dining area open to the outdoors and you have the perfect layout for casual family living. Also, a convenient utility room is adjacent to the garage so muddy chores don't make their way into the house. Retreat to the master bedroom featuring a private bath, dressing area and access to the large covered porch perfect for unwinding after a long, hard day.

Price Code B

Plan #587-005D-0001

Total Square Feet -1,400

Bedrooms - 3
Baths - 2
Garage - 2-car

Foundation - Basement foundation, drawings also include crawl space

A terrific front facade is achieved with the help of roof dormers adding great curb appeal. Plus, the charming covered front porch provides an outdoor seating area perfect for warm days and nights. Inside the home, the living room and master bedroom feature vaulted ceilings and the master bedroom is secluded for privacy. Two other great features are the large utility room containing additional cabinet space and the oversized garage with storage space.

Price Code B

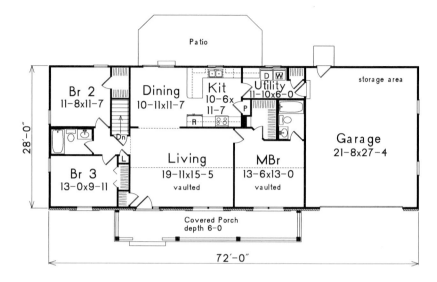

Total Square Feet - 2,029

Bedrooms - 4

Baths - 2

Garage - 2-car side entry

Foundation - Basement, drawings also include crawl space and slab

Stonework, gables, roof dormer and double porches create a country flavor to the exterior. The kitchen enjoys extravagant cabinetry, a counterspace in a bay, island snack bar, built-in pantry and a cheery dining area with multiple tall windows. Angled stairs descend from a large entry with wood columns and is open to a vaulted great room with a corner fireplace. Relax in the master bedroom boasting two walk-in closets, a private bath with double-door entry and a secluded porch.

Price Code D

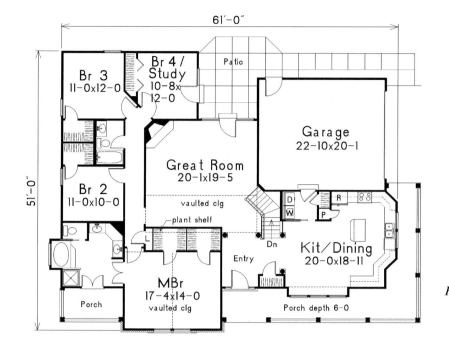

- 61'-0"
- 51'-0"
- Br 3 11-0x12-0
- Br 4/ Study 10-8x12-0
- Patio
- Garage 22-10x20-1
- Great Room 20-1x19-5
- vaulted clg
- plant shelf
- Br 2 11-0x10-0
- L
- Dn
- D W P R
- Kit/Dining 20-0x18-11
- Entry
- MBr 17-4x14-0 vaulted clg
- Porch
- Porch depth 6-0

Plan #587-001D-0024

Total Square Feet - 1,360

Bedrooms - 3
Baths - 2
Garage - 2-car side entry

Foundation - Basement, drawings
also include crawl space and slab

Organized living is easy with the
extras found throughout this home to
keep everything in place. The
kitchen/dining room features an
island workspace and plenty of
dining area with an adjacent laundry
room. Of course, the master bedroom
has a large walk-in closet and private
bath, but large closets also adorn
the secondary bedrooms maintaining
organization for each member of the
family. The high function continues
in the garage where a convenient
workshop can be found.

Price Code A

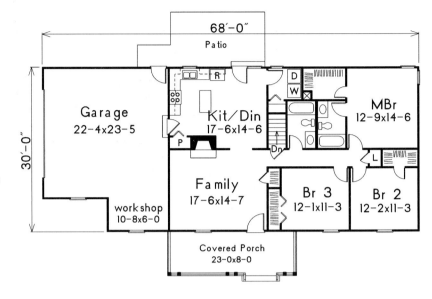

Total Square Feet - 1,791
Bedrooms - 4
Baths - 2
Garage - 2-car with storage

*Foundation - Basement, drawings
also include crawl space and slab*

*Stunning windows grace the
interior of this home everywhere
you look. The vaulted great room
and octagon-shaped dining area
enjoy a spectacular view of the
covered patio through several
windows. Meanwhile, the kitchen
features a pass-through to the dining
area, a center island, a large walk-
in pantry and breakfast room that
once again, has a large bay window.
In addition, the master bedroom is
vaulted with a sitting area
bathed in sunlight.*

Price Code C

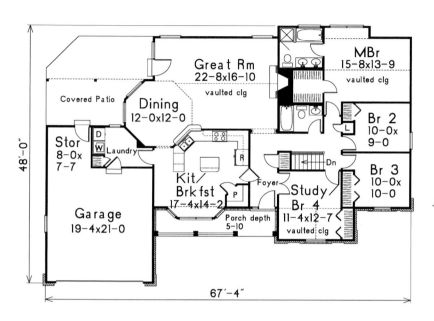

Plan #587-053D-0002

Total Square Feet - 1,668
Bedrooms - 3
Baths - 2
Garage - 2-car drive under
Foundation - Basement

Bay windows throughout make this home shine. Large bay windows grace the breakfast area, master bedroom and dining room. The large living room has a fireplace, built-in bookshelves and a sloped ceiling adding even more comfortable living to this plan. Plus, extensive walk-in closets and storage spaces are located throughout the home perfect for keeping everything in its place.

Price Code C

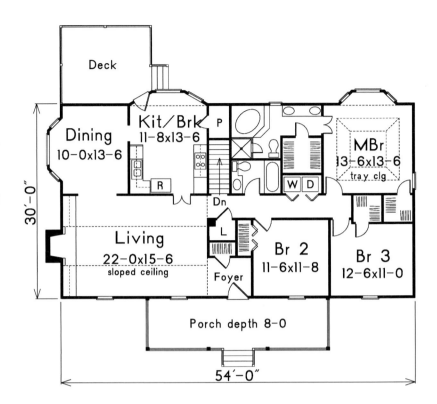

Plan #587-007D-0060

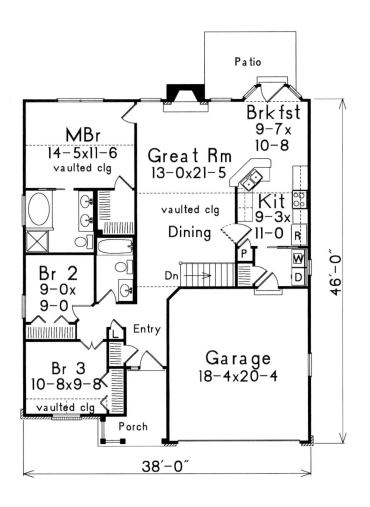

Total Square Feet - 1,268
Bedrooms - 3
Baths - 2
Garage - 2-car

*Foundation - Basement, drawings
also include crawl space and slab*

*Multiple gables, a covered porch
and arched windows create a classy
exterior while innovative interior
design provides openness in the great
room, kitchen and breakfast room.
A vaulted ceiling is enjoyed by the
master bedroom and the secondary
bedrooms have a
private hall with bath.*

Price Code B

Plan #587-055D-0017

Total Square Feet - 1,525

Bedrooms - 3
Baths - 2
Garage - 2-car

Foundation - Basement, walk-out basement, crawl space or slab, please specify when ordering

The great room is highlighted with an open bar and a fireplace. Cheerful and bright, the breakfast room leads to an outdoor grilling and covered porch perfect for enjoying alfresco dining during pleasant seasons. Extra amenities can also be found in the master bath which features a unique glass block window over the whirlpool tub.

Price Code B

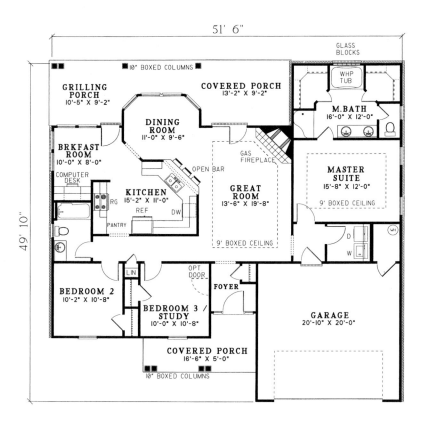

Plan #587-035D-0045

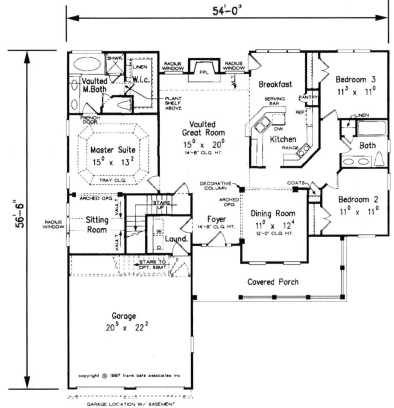

54'-0"

56'-6"

Vaulted M.Bath

SHWR.

LINEN

RADIUS WINDOW

FPL

RADIUS WINDOW

W.i.c.

Breakfast

Bedroom 3
11³ x 11⁰

PLANT SHELF ABOVE

SERVING BAR

PANTRY

FRENCH DOOR

Vaulted Great Room
15⁰ x 20⁰
14'-6" CLG. HT.

REF.

DW

Kitchen

LINEN

Master Suite
15⁰ x 13²

TRAY CLG.

RANGE

Bath

DECORATIVE COLUMN

COATS

RADIUS WINDOW

ARCHED OPG.

VAULT

STAIRS UP

Sitting Room

VAULT

W.

D.

ARCHED OPG.

Foyer
14'-6" CLG. HT.

Dining Room
11⁰ x 12⁴
12'-0" CLG. HT.

Bedroom 2
11⁰ x 11⁰

Laund.

VAULT

STAIRS TO OPT. BSMT.

Covered Porch

Garage
20⁵ x 22²

copyright © 1997 frank betz associates, inc.

GARAGE LOCATION W/ BASEMENT

Total Square Feet - 1,749

Bedrooms - 3

Baths - 2

Garage - 2-car

Foundation - Slab, crawl space or walk-out basement, please specify when ordering

Upon entering, view the breathtaking great room, dining room and kitchen. A private master suite is topped with an elegant tray ceiling and includes a bath and cozy sitting room. Additional bedrooms are located away from the master suite ensuring privacy. An optional bonus room above the garage has an additional 308 square feet of living area.

Price Code B

Plan #587-007D-0067

Total Square Feet - 1,761

Bedrooms - 4

Baths - 2

Garage - 2-car side entry

Foundation - Basement

Exterior window dressing, roof dormers and planter boxes provide visual warmth and charm to the front facade. Inside, the great room boasts a vaulted ceiling, fireplace and opens to a pass-through kitchen. Also, the vaulted master bedroom includes a luxury bath and walk-in closet making the room the perfect retreat. Plus, this home features eight separate closets with an abundance of storage.

Price Code B

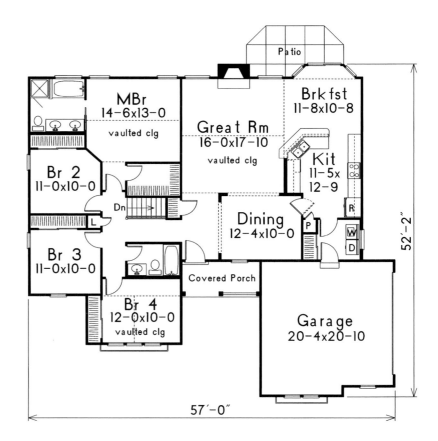

Total Square Feet - 1,708
Bedrooms - 3
Baths - 2
Garage - 2-car

Foundation - Basement, drawings
also include crawl space

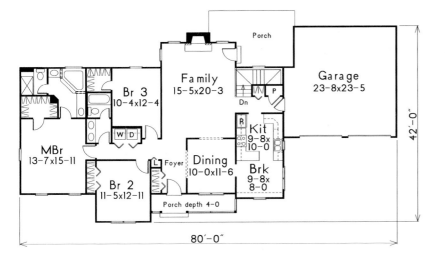

The massive family room is enhanced with several windows, a fireplace and access to the porch. Lots of amenities are included in the more private areas of the home as well, such as the deluxe master bath which is accented by a step-up corner tub flanked by double vanities or large closets throughout that help to maintain organized living. Plus, all the bedrooms are isolated from the living areas for a more private feel.

Price Code B

Plan #587-033D-0012

Total Square Feet - 1,546

Bedrooms - 3
Baths - 2
Garage - 2-car
Foundation - Basement

Spacious, open rooms provide a casual atmosphere creating a friendly feel to this home. The kitchen and dinette combine for added space and include access to the outdoors. While the more formal dining room features an exceptional bay window. A large laundry room includes a convenient sink making the household chores easy and efficient.

Price Code C

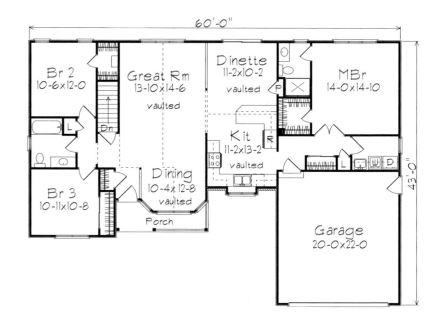

Total Square Feet - 1,787

Bedrooms - 3
Baths - 2
Garage - 2-car side entry

Foundation - Basement, crawl space
or slab, please specify when ordering

Skylights brighten the screen porch
which connects to the family room
and deck outdoors. An adjacent
kitchen has a serving bar which
extends dining into the family room.
Comfort is also enjoyed in the master
bedroom featuring a lovely sitting
area, large private bath and direct
access to the screen porch.

Price Code B

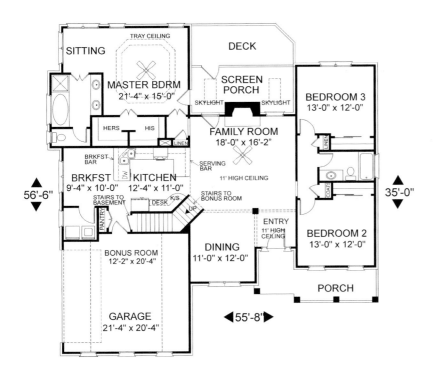

Plan #587-007D-0068

Total Square Feet - 1,384
Bedrooms - 2
Baths - 2
Garage - 1-car side entry
Foundation - Walk-out basement

The wrap-around country front porch is perfect for peaceful evenings. Inside, the vaulted great room enjoys a large bay window, a stone fireplace, a pass-through counter from the kitchen and awesome rear views through an atrium window wall. The master bedroom features a double-door entry, walk-in closet and a fabulous bath offering the perfect environment for relaxation after a long day. 611 square feet of optional living area is available in the atrium below offering more casual living space.

Price Code B

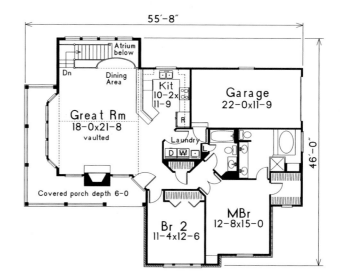

First Floor - 1,384 sq. ft.

Optional Lower Level - 611 sq. ft.

Rear View

57'-0"

56'-4"

Covered Porch

Vaulted Sitting Area

Breakfast

FRENCH DOOR

FPL.

VAULT

VAULT

Bedroom 2
12⁶ x 10⁴

Master Suite
17⁰ x 13⁰
TRAY CLG.

TRAY CLG.

SERVING BAR

RANGE

D.W.

Kitchen

Vaulted Family Room
15⁰ x 20⁷
14'-0" HIGH CEILING

Bath

PANTRY

REF.

NICHE

LIN.

K.S.

Vaulted M.Bath

PLANT SHELF ABOVE

COATS

Laund.

W.

D.

Foyer
14'-0" HIGH CLG.

DECORATIVE COLUMNS

PLANT SHELF ABOVE

W.i.c.

LINEN

SHWR.

Covered Entry

Dining Room
12⁵ x 12⁷
14'-0" HIGH CEILING

Bedroom 3
10⁶ x 12⁰

Garage
22⁵ x 20²

copyright © 1995 frank betz associates, inc.

Total Square Feet - 1,779

Bedrooms - 3

Baths - 2

Garage - 2-car

Foundation - Walk-out basement, slab or crawl space, please specify when ordering

This well-designed floor plan has a vaulted family room with fireplace and access to the outdoors. Neat touches like decorative columns separate the dining area from the foyer in a pleasant and interesting way. A vaulted ceiling adds spaciousness in the master bath that also features a walk-in closet.

Price Code B

Plan #587-040D-0003

Total Square Feet - 1,475

Bedrooms - 3

Baths - 2

Garage - 2-car detached side entry

Foundation - Slab, drawings also
include crawl space

A covered breezeway joins the main
house to the garage and a full-width
covered porch entry lends a country
touch to the exterior. Inside, the
family room features a high ceiling
and prominent corner fireplace.
An efficient kitchen with island
counter and garden window makes
a convenient connection between the
family and dining rooms. One long
hallway leads to three bedrooms all
with large walk-in closets.

Price Code B

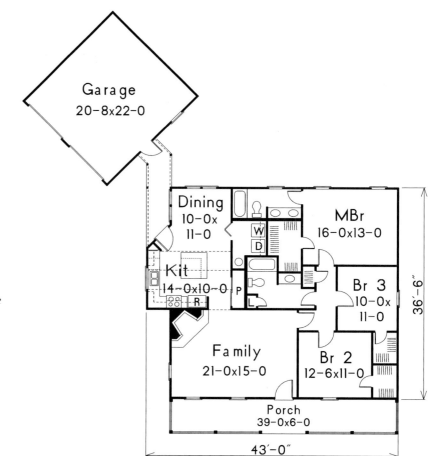

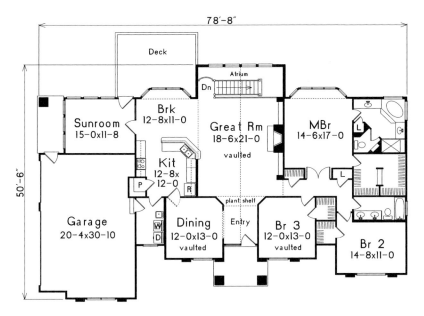

First Floor - 2,397 sq. ft.

Deck

Sunroom
15-0x11-8

Brk
12-8x11-0

Atrium
Dn

Great Rm
18-6x21-0
vaulted

MBr
14-6x17-0

Kit
12-8x
12-0

Garage
20-4x30-10

plant shelf

Dining
12-0x13-0
vaulted

Entry

Br 3
12-0x13-0
vaulted

Br 2
14-8x11-0

78'-8"

50'-6"

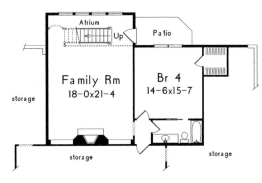

Optional Lower Level - 898 sq. ft.

Atrium
Up

Patio

Family Rm
18-0x21-4

Br 4
14-6x15-7

storage

storage

storage

Total Square Feet - 2,397

Bedrooms - 3

Baths - 2

Garage - 3-car side entry

Foundation - Walk-out basement

A grand entry porch leads to a dramatic vaulted foyer with plant shelf open to a great room which enjoys a 12' vaulted ceiling, an atrium featuring 2 1/2 story windows and a fireplace with flanking bookshelves. A conveniently located sunroom and side porch adjoin the breakfast room and garage effortlessly. Add 898 square feet of optional living area on the lower level with a family room, bedroom #4 and bath and you have the flexibility a growing family needs.

Price Code D

Plan #587-058D-0016

Total Square Feet - 1,558

Bedrooms - 3
Baths - 2
Garage - 2-car
Foundation - Basement

The spacious utility room is located conveniently between the garage and kitchen/dining area. An enormous living area with fireplace and vaulted ceiling opens to the kitchen and dining area creating a sense of openness throughout the home. The bedrooms are separated from the living area by a hallway with a master bedroom enhanced with a large bay window, walk-in closet and private bath.

Price Code B

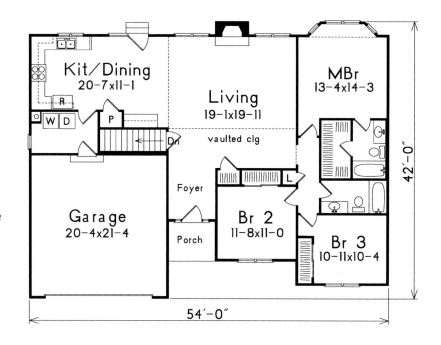

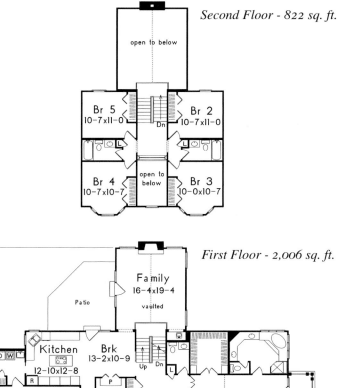

Second Floor - 822 sq. ft.

open to below

Br 5
10-7x11-0

Br 2
10-7x11-0

Dn

L

L

Br 4
10-7x10-7

open to below

Br 3
10-0x10-7

Total Square Feet - 2,828

Bedrooms - 5

Baths - 3 1/2

Garage - 2-car side entry

*Foundation - Basement, drawings
also include crawl space and slab*

*A popular wrap-around porch
gives this home country charm.
A secluded, oversized family room
with vaulted ceiling and wet bar
features many windows providing
an inviting and friendly interior
space. Any chef would be delighted to
cook in this smartly designed kitchen
with island and corner windows.
Plus, this home has a spectacular
master bedroom and bath.*

Price Code F

First Floor - 2,006 sq. ft.

Family
16-4x19-4
vaulted

Patio

Kitchen
12-10x12-8

D W

R

Brk
13-2x10-9

Up Dn

L

55'-6"

Garage
20-4x21-10

Dining
12-2x13-0

P

Foyer

Study
13-5x13-0

MBr
15-0x16-11
vaulted

Porch depth 6-0

70'-6"

Plan #587-035D-0036

Total Square Feet - 2,193

Bedrooms - 3

Baths - 3

Garage - 2-car side entry

Foundation - Walk-out basement, crawl space or slab, please specify when ordering

A distinctive dining room has decorative columns and overlooks the family room. The kitchen has lots of storage keeping the area from appearing cluttered. An exquisite master suite includes a sitting room for a private escape. With the addition of an optional 400 square foot bonus room with bath on the second floor, this home has everything you could ask for.

Price Code C

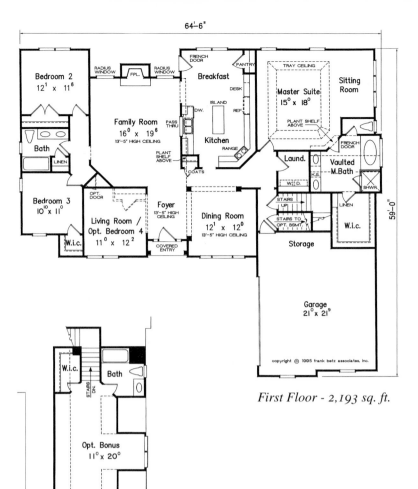

First Floor - 2,193 sq. ft.

Optional Second Floor - 400 sq. ft.

Total Square Feet - 1,550
Bedrooms - 3
Baths - 2
Garage - 2-car
Foundation - Slab

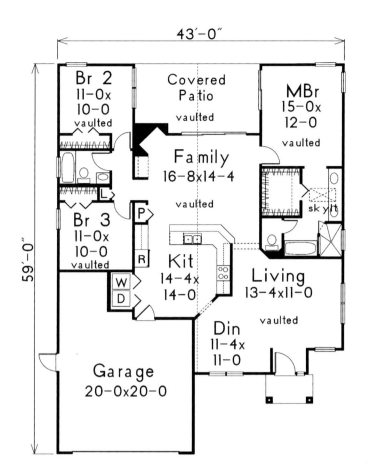

43'-0"

Br 2
11-0x
10-0
vaulted

Covered
Patio
vaulted

MBr
15-0x
12-0
vaulted

Family
16-8x14-4
vaulted

skylt

Br 3
11-0x
10-0
vaulted

P
R

Kit
14-4x
14-0

Living
13-4x11-0
vaulted

59'-0"

W
D

Din
11-4x
11-0

Garage
20-0x20-0

Flexibility allows the alcove in the family room to be used as a cozy corner fireplace or as a media center depending on your needs. The kitchen with pantry and breakfast bar connects to the family room with a convenient laundry closet nearby. A private master bedroom features a large walk-in closet, skylight and separate tub and shower. Plus, both the family room and master bedroom access the covered patio offering plenty of flexibility and accessibility.

Price Code B

Plan #587-007D-0017

Total Square Feet - 1,882

Bedrooms - 4
Baths - 2
Garage - 2-car side entry
Foundation - Basement

A handsome brick facade covers the front of this home. Step inside to find a spacious great room and dining area combination brightened by unique corner windows and patio access. The well-designed kitchen incorporates a breakfast bar peninsula, a sweeping casement window above the sink and a walk-in pantry island. In addition, a master bedroom features a large walk-in closet and private bath with bay window.

Price Code C

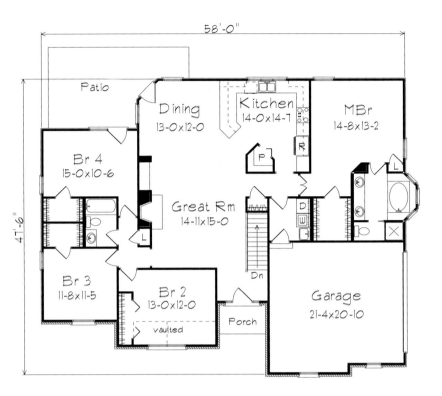

Total Square Feet - 1,285

Bedrooms - 3
Baths - 2
Foundation - Crawl space, drawings
also include basement and slab

*Accommodating home with
ranch-style porch makes outdoor
living easily accessible. The kitchen
features a pantry, breakfast bar
and complete view to the dining
room. The master bedroom includes
a dressing area, private bath and
built-in bookcase. Perfect for lawn
equipment and other items, a large
storage area on the back of the home
provides a place for odds and ends.*

Price Code B

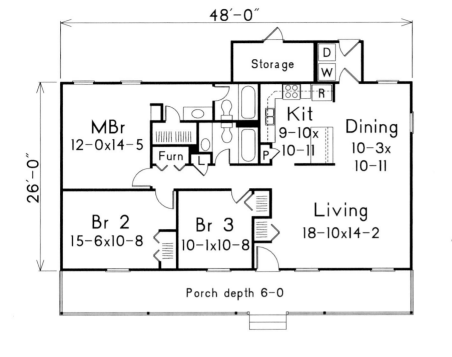

Plan #587-035D-0032

Total Square Feet - 1,856

Bedrooms - 3

Baths - 2

Garage - 2-car side entry

Foundation - Walk-out basement, crawl space or slab, please specify when ordering

A beautiful covered porch creates a Southern accent to the exterior of this home. Upon entering you'll discover a large foyer with a grand entrance leading into the family room through columns and an arched opening. When you see the kitchen you'll notice it has an organized feel with plenty of cabinetry.

Price Code C

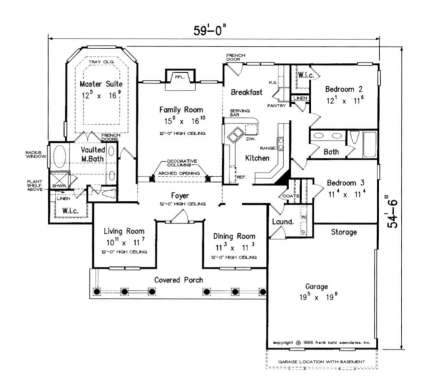

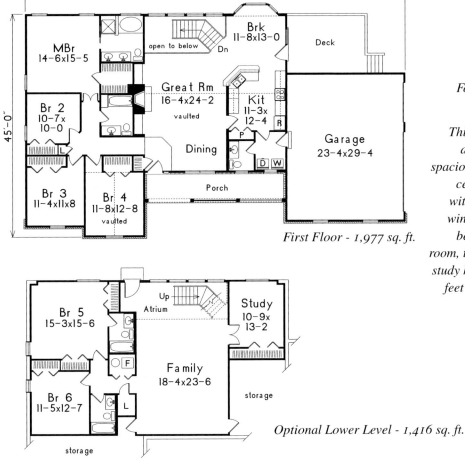

First Floor - 1,977 sq. ft.

Optional Lower Level - 1,416 sq. ft.

Total Square Feet - 1,977

Bedrooms - 4

Baths - 2 1/2

Garage - 3-car side entry

Foundation - Walk-out basement

This classic traditional exterior is always in style. A gorgeous and spacious great room boasts a vaulted ceiling, a dining area, an atrium with elegant staircase and feature windows. The optional living area below which consists of a family room, two bedrooms, two baths and a study has an additional 1,416 square feet of living area perfect for older children or an in-law suite.

Price Code C

Plan #587-053D-0030

Total Square Feet - 1,657

Bedrooms - 3
Baths - 2 1/2
Garage - 2-car drive under
Foundation - Basement

The stylish pass-through between the living and dining areas keeps the first floor highly functional and stylish. Large windows in the breakfast and dining areas encourage a cheerful environment. Meanwhile, the master bedroom can be found secluded from the living areas for well-deserved privacy.

Price Code B

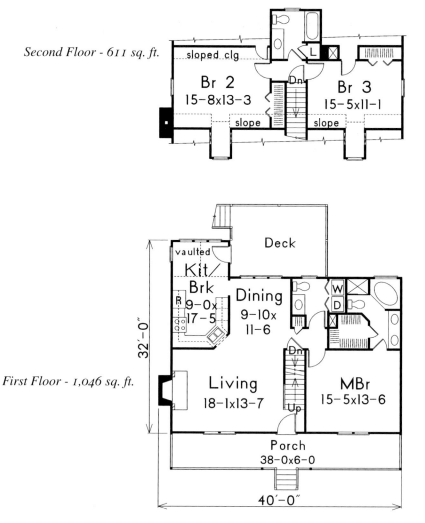

Second Floor - 611 sq. ft.

First Floor - 1,046 sq. ft.

Second Floor - 773 sq. ft.

MBr
12-0x14-8
vaulted clg
Br 2
12-0x11-0
Dn
L
Br 3
12-0x11-3
vaulted clg

plant shelf

36'-0"

46'-8"

First Floor - 802 sq. ft.

Kit
9-0x11-7
Brk fst
10-0x11-0
Dining
12-0x11-0
R
Dn
D W P
Up
Living
15-7x14-4
Garage
19-4x20-4

Total Square Feet - 1,575
Bedrooms - 3
Baths - 2 1/2
Garage - 2-car

Foundation - Basement, drawings
also include crawl space and slab

An inviting porch leads to
both spacious living and dining
rooms. The kitchen with
corner windows features an island
snack bar, an attractive breakfast
room bay, a convenient laundry area
and a built-in pantry. More amenities
adorn the master bedroom suite
which features a private bath and
a large walk-in closet.

Price Code B

Plan #587-035D-0048

Total Square Feet - 1,915

Bedrooms - 4
Baths - 3
Garage - 2-car

Foundation - Walk-out basement, slab
or crawl space, please specify when
ordering

A large breakfast area overlooks the
vaulted great room creating a true
sense of openness. It's easy to enjoy
the master suite that has a cheerful
sitting room and private bath within
its walls. This terrific plan features a
unique in-law suite with private bath
and walk-in closet allowing future
flexibility when needed.

Price Code C

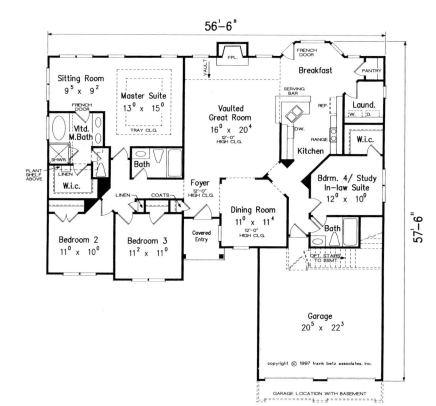

Total Square Feet - 1,170
Bedrooms - 3
Baths - 2
Garage - 2-car
Foundation - Slab

The living areas of this home combine to create a greater sense of spaciousness. The great room has a cozy fireplace while the kitchen has an angled bar that overlooks the great room and breakfast area in a favorable way. Remaining secluded, the master bedroom enjoys privacy at the rear of this home.

Price Code AA

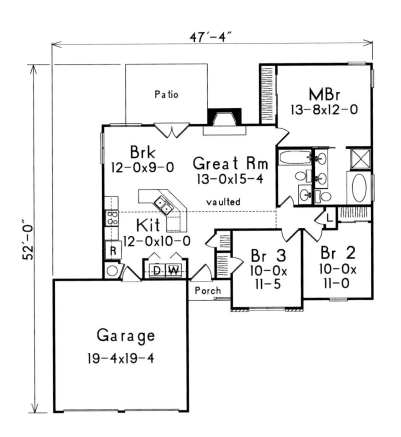

Plan #587-007D-0058

Total Square Feet - 4,826

Bedrooms - 4
Baths - 3 1/2
Garage - 3-car side entry

Foundation - Walk-out basement with lawn and garden workroom

A brightly lit entry connects to the great room with balcony and massive bay-shaped atrium. The kitchen has an island/snack bar, walk-in pantry, computer area and an atrium overlook. Step inside the master bedroom and find a sitting area, walk-in closets, an atrium overlook and luxury bath with private courtyard. A family room/atrium, home theater area with wet bar, game room and guest bedroom comprise the lower level.

Price Code G

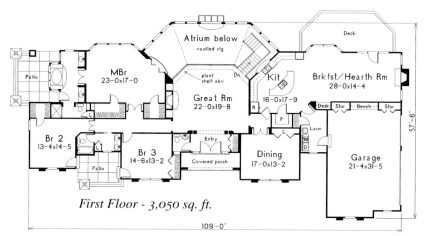

First Floor - 3,050 sq. ft.

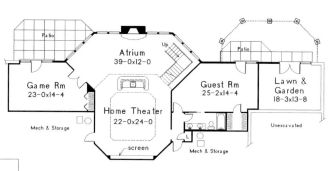

Lower Level - 1,776 sq. ft.

Great Room/Atrium Interior View

Second Floor - 946 sq. ft.

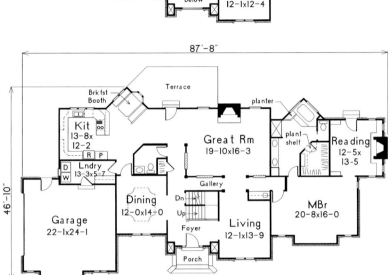

First Floor - 2,276 sq. ft.

Total Square Feet - 3,222

Bedrooms - 4
Baths - 3 1/2
Garage - 2-car side entry

Foundation - Basement, drawings
also include crawl space and slab

*Enter this home to discover a
two-story foyer featuring a central
staircase and views to the second
floor, dining and living rooms.
Nearby a built-in breakfast booth is
surrounded by windows creating a
friendly atmosphere for dining. The
gourmet kitchen includes a view to
the two-story great room featuring
a large fireplace and arched
openings to the second floor. Also,
an elegant master bedroom has
a separate reading room with
bookshelves and fireplace.*

Price Code F

Plan #587-062D-0050

Total Square Feet - 1,408

Bedrooms - 3
Baths - 2
Garage - 2-car side entry

Foundation - Basement or crawl space, please specify when ordering

The front entry is sheltered by a broad veranda which leads directly into the informal great room. Towards the rear of the home you'll find a bright country kitchen that boasts an abundance of counterspace and cupboards perfect for maintaining an organized feel. Special touches have also been added to the master bath which has a spa tub brightened by a box-bay window.

Price Code A

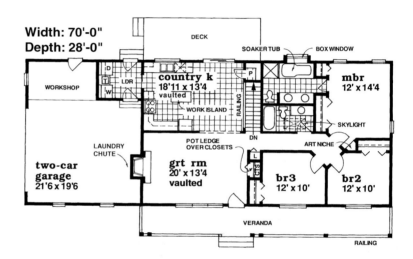

Width: 70'-0"
Depth: 28'-0"

Plan #587-007D-0008

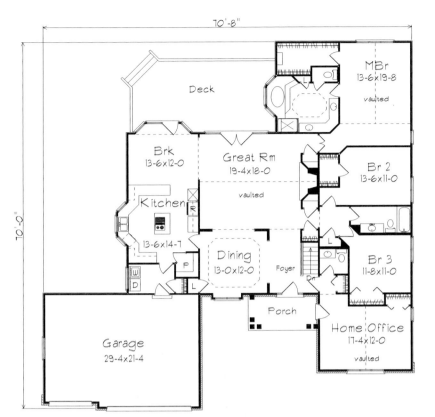

Total Square Feet - 2,452
Bedrooms - 3
Baths - 2 1/2
Garage - 3-car
Foundation - Basement

Delightful great room features a vaulted ceiling, a fireplace, extra storage closets and patio doors to the sundeck. In addition, a cheery and spacious home office with private entrance and bath has two closets, a vaulted ceiling and transomed window perfect as shown or used as a fourth bedroom. The extra-large kitchen features a walk-in pantry, cooktop island and bay window. Luxury can also be found in the vaulted master bedroom including transomed windows, a walk-in closet and a deluxe bath.

Price Code D

Plan #587-004D-0002

Total Square Feet - 1,823

Bedrooms - 3

Baths - 2

Garage - 2-car

Foundation - Basement

A terrific 6' deep wrap-around porch offers the opportunity for outdoor living accessible from the living and dining rooms. Upon entering the vaulted living room, you'll find a large space that easily accesses the dining area. The cheerful dining area is convenient to the U-shaped kitchen and also enjoys patio access for outdoor dining. More convenience will be enjoyed with a centrally located laundry room connecting the garage to the living areas. Luxury is achieved in the master bedroom boasting a tray ceiling, a large walk-in closet and a private bath with a corner whirlpool tub.

Price Code C

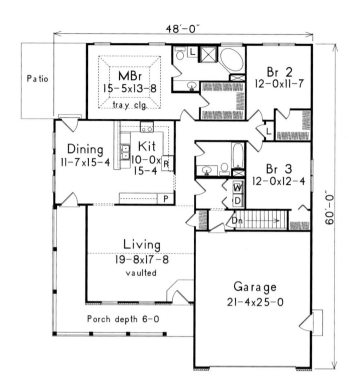

Total Square Feet - 1,220
Bedrooms - 3
Baths - 2
Garage - 2-car drive under
Foundation - Basement

The covered porch entry adds appeal to the front facade, while the rear deck adjoins the gracious dining area that is adjacent to the convenient wrap-around kitchen. The spacious living room is accented with a large fireplace and hearth. With the washer and dryer handy to the bedrooms, there no doubt will be ease with household chores. The vaulted ceiling adds equal luxury to both the living room and master bedroom.

Price Code A

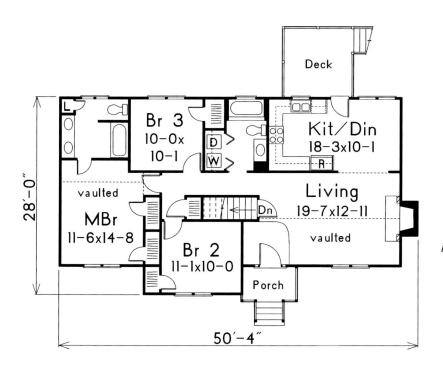

Plan #587-035D-0035

Total Square Feet - 2,322

Bedrooms - 3
Baths - 2 1/2
Garage - 2-car side entry
Foundation - Walk-out basement,
crawl space or slab, please specify
when ordering

This well-designed floor plan offers
unique extras creating a custom feel
throughout. Decorative columns and
arched openings surround the dining
area adding a remarkably plush
feel. The vaulted family room has a
fireplace and access to the kitchen
which includes an island with a
serving bar. Luxury is defined in the
master suite featuring a sitting room
and grand-scale bath.

Price Code D

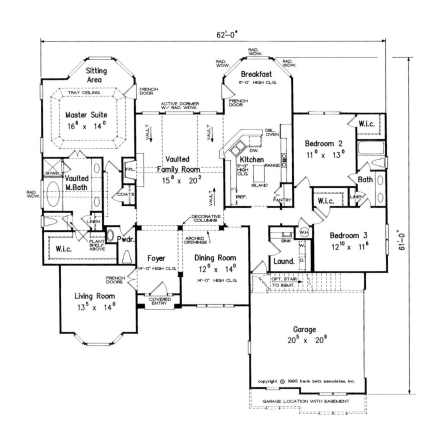

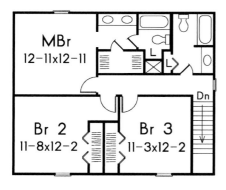

MBr
12-11x12-11

Br 2
11-8x12-2

Br 3
11-3x12-2

Dn

Second Floor - 832 sq. ft.

Total Square Feet - 1,664

Bedrooms - 3
Baths - 2 1/2
Garage - 2-car

*Foundation - Crawl space, drawings
also include basement and slab*

*Modest family living makes this
home a winner. The L-shaped
country kitchen includes a pantry
and a cozy breakfast area.
All bedrooms are located on the
second floor for privacy. While the
master bedroom receives special
pampering with a walk-in closet,
dressing area and bath.*

Price Code B

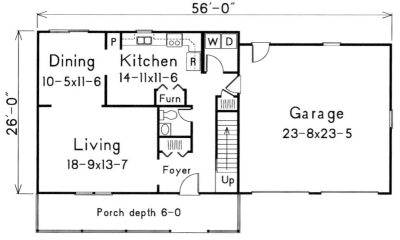

56'-0"

26'-0"

P
Dining
10-5x11-6

Kitchen
14-11x11-6

W D
R

Furn

Living
18-9x13-7

Foyer

Up

Garage
23-8x23-5

Porch depth 6-0

First Floor - 832 sq. ft.

Plan #587-055D-0030

Total Square Feet - 2,107

Bedrooms - 4
Baths - 2 1/2
Garage - 2-car

Foundation - Crawl space, basement, walk-out basement or slab, please specify when ordering

Upon entering this home you'll discover a centralized great room warmed by a fireplace and featuring easy access to any area in the home. Adjacent to the great room, a spacious breakfast room and kitchen include a center island with eating space ideal for casual dining. Another plus to this design is the master bedroom which is separate from other bedrooms for privacy.

Price Code C

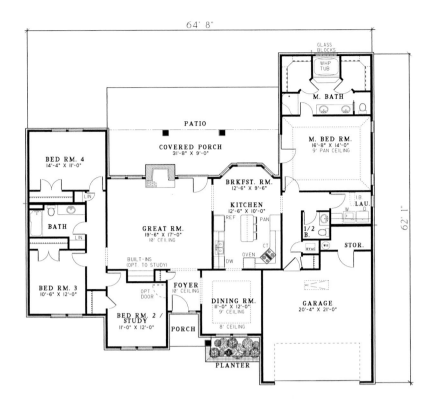

Plan #587-027D-0005

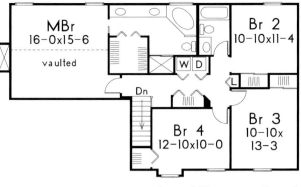

Second Floor - 1,108 sq. ft.

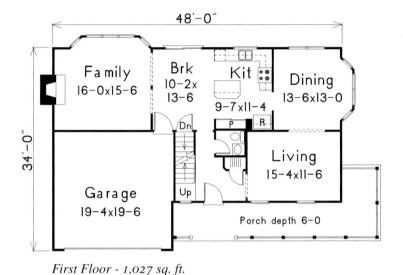

First Floor - 1,027 sq. ft.

Total Square Feet - 2,135

Bedrooms - 4
Baths - 2 1/2
Garage - 2-car

Foundation - Basement

Formal living and dining rooms add elegance and style to the home. The enormous family room features an impressive fireplace and full wall of windows that joins the breakfast room creating a spacious gathering area. The chef of the home will love the ease of the kitchen which features an island counter and pantry. The second floor houses the private bedrooms with a nearby washer and dryer making this household chore a breeze.

Price Code D

Plan #587-039D-0001

Total Square Feet - 1,253

Bedrooms - 3
Baths - 2
Garage - 2-car

Foundation - Crawl space or slab, please specify when ordering

The spacious family room with sloped ceiling and fireplace offers a dramatic first impression in this charming home. The U-shaped kitchen is efficiently designed keeping everything within reach and opening to the large dining room and rear porch. The bedrooms are located in the right wing of the home for added privacy and they all enjoy large walk-in closets.

Price Code A

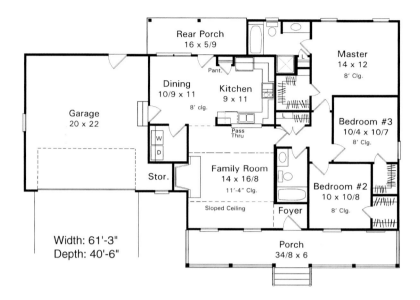

Garage
20 x 22

Rear Porch
16 x 5/9

Dining
10/9 x 11
8' clg.

Kitchen
9 x 11

Pant.

Master
14 x 12
8' Clg.

Bedroom #3
10/4 x 10/7
8' Clg.

Pass Thru

W
D

Stor.

Family Room
14 x 16/8
11'-4" Clg.

Sloped Ceiling

Foyer

Bedroom #2
10 x 10/8
8' Clg.

Width: 61'-3"
Depth: 40'-6"

Porch
34/8 x 6

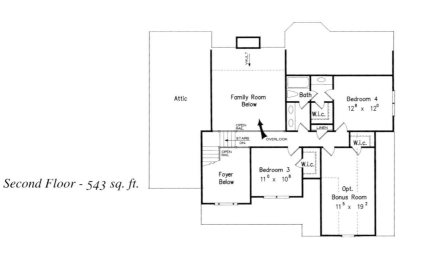

Second Floor - 543 sq. ft.

Total Square Feet - 2,126

Bedrooms - 4
Baths - 3
Garage - 2-car side entry

Foundation - Walk-out basement, crawl space or slab, please specify when ordering

The breathtaking two-story foyer creates an airy feeling and welcomes all into the home. The kitchen overlooks the vaulted family room with a handy serving bar perfect for quick meals or serving buffet-style dinners. Adding flexibility to the plan, the second floor includes an optional bonus room with an additional 251 square feet of living area.

Price Code C

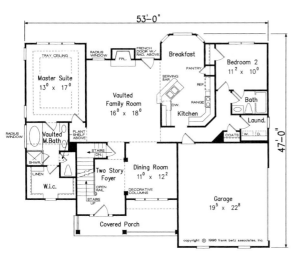

First Floor - 1,583 sq. ft.

Plan #587-007D-0089

Total Square Feet - 2,125

Bedrooms - 3

Baths - 2 1/2

Garage - 2-car side entry

Foundation - Walk-out basement

A cozy front porch leads to the vaulted great room with fireplace through the entry which has a walk-in closet and bath. The large and well-arranged kitchen offers spectacular views from its cantilevered sink cabinetry through a two-story atrium window wall. The left side of the home is for relaxing with the master bedroom boasting a sitting room, large walk-in closet and bath with garden tub overhanging a brightly lit atrium. The lower level includes 1,047 square feet of optional living area with a study and family room with walk-in bar and full bath.

Price Code C

First Floor - 2,125 sq. ft.

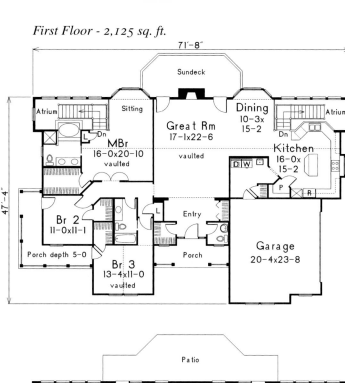

Optional Lower Level - 1,047 sq. ft.

Plan #587-035D-0050

Total Square Feet -1,342

Bedrooms - 3

Baths - 2

Garage - 2-car

Foundation - Slab, walk-out basement or crawl space, please specify when ordering

This spacious ranch features 9' ceilings throughout to increase the open feel. The master suite is a relaxing retreat with a tray ceiling and wall of windows that overlooks the backyard. The dining room includes a serving bar connecting it to the kitchen and sliding glass doors that lead outdoors. With an abundance of amenities, including a 350 square foot optional bonus room, this home will truly please.

Price Code A

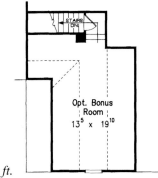

Optional Second Floor - 350 sq. ft.

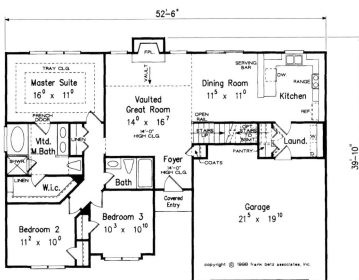

First Floor - 1,342 sq. ft.

Plan #587-020D-0015

Total Square Feet - 1,191

Bedrooms - 3

Baths - 2

Garage - 2-car side entry

Foundation - Slab, drawings also include crawl space

Designed with style and beauty from the inside out, this home is also designed to be energy efficient with 2" x 6" exterior walls perfect for maintaining economical heating and cooling costs year-round. The impressive living room offers a grand first impression of the home with a cathedral ceiling and stone fireplace. The secluded master bedroom is a welcomed escape with a lavish dressing area and private bath.

Price Code AA

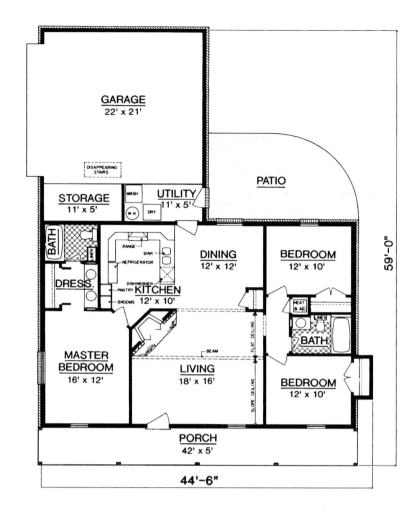

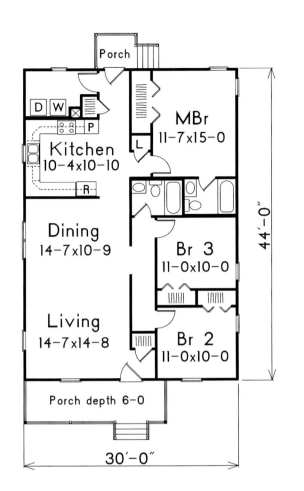

Porch

D W

P

Kitchen
10-4x10-10

L

MBr
11-7x15-0

R

Dining
14-7x10-9

Br 3
11-0x10-0

Living
14-7x14-8

Br 2
11-0x10-0

44'-0"

Porch depth 6-0

30'-0"

Total Square Feet - 1,320

Bedrooms - 3

Baths - 2

Foundation - Crawl space

A charming covered front porch invites guests and opens into a large living area with a convenient coat closet. The functional U-shaped kitchen features a convenient pantry. The spacious living and dining areas join to create an open atmosphere, perfect for relaxing or entertaining. Behind the kitchen, a laundry room is housed with access to the back porch. This home fits well on a narrow lot and provides all of the amenities one needs.

Price Code A

Plan #587-035D-0056

Total Square Feet - 2,246

Bedrooms - 4

Baths - 3

Garage - 2-car side entry

Foundation - Walk-out basement, slab or crawl space, please specify when ordering

Brick and a charming turret enhance the exterior while the two-story foyer offers a grand first impression of the interior. To the left of the foyer is the master suite which features a sitting area with bay window. The centrally located kitchen serves the bayed breakfast area and formal dining room. Bedroom #4 easily converts to an office allowing for flexible planning. The second floor includes two secondary bedrooms that share a full bath and an optional bonus room which has an additional 269 square feet of living area.

Price Code D

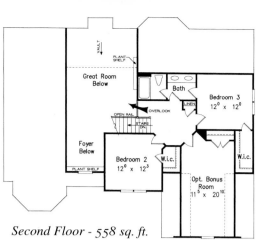

Second Floor - 558 sq. ft.

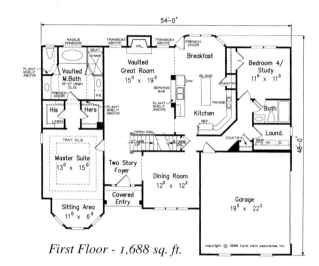

First Floor - 1,688 sq. ft.

Second Floor - 1,069 sq. ft.

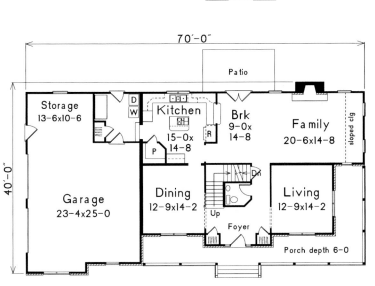

Plan #587-004D-0001

Total Square Feet - 2,505
Bedrooms - 3
Baths - 2 1/2
Garage - 2-car side entry

*Foundation - Basement, drawings
also include crawl space*

This country charmer welcomes guests with a wrap-around porch and spacious foyer. Inside, formal living and dining rooms provide ample space for entertaining or quiet intimate gatherings. An efficient kitchen includes a walk-in pantry and opens to the breakfast and family rooms for an open atmosphere. The bedrooms are located on the second floor with the master bedroom featuring a bath with a deluxe raised tub and immense walk-in closet. The garage features extra storage area and ample workspace perfect for any handyman.

First Floor - 1,436 sq. ft.

Price Code D

Plan #587-001D-0013

Total Square Feet - 1,882

Bedrooms - 3
Baths - 2
Garage - 2-car

Foundation - Basement

This best-selling ranch starts things off right with a wide, handsome entrance opening to the vaulted great room with fireplace. The great room and dining area are conveniently joined but still allow privacy. A private covered porch extends the breakfast area allowing easy meals to be taken outdoors. A practical passageway runs through the laundry room from the garage to the kitchen. A vaulted ceiling tops the master bedroom creating an enchanting atmosphere.

Price Code D

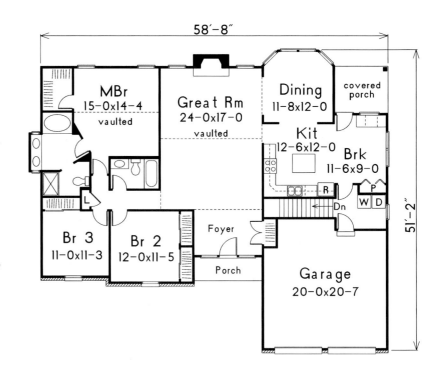

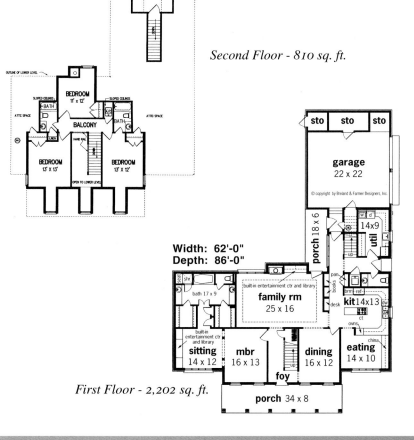

FUTURE SPACE
28' x 12'
SLOPED CEILINGS

Second Floor - 810 sq. ft.

BEDROOM
11' x 12'

BALCONY

BEDROOM
13' x 13'

BEDROOM
13' X 12'

sto sto sto

garage
22 x 22

© copyright by Breland & Farmer Designers, Inc.

porch 18 x 6

14x9

util

Width: 62'-0"
Depth: 86'-0"

bath 17 x 9

built-in entertainment ctr and library

family rm
25 x 16

kit 14x13

built-in
entertainment ctr
and library

sitting
14 x 12

mbr
16 x 13

dining
16 x 12

eating
14 x 10

foy

First Floor - 2,202 sq. ft.

porch 34 x 8

Total Square Feet - 3,012

Bedrooms - 4
Baths - 3 1/2
Garage - 2-car side entry
Foundation - Crawl space, drawings
also include slab and basement

The ultimate in luxury has been achieved in the master bedroom which features a sitting area with an entertainment center/library sure to be a terrific place for unwinding after a long day. Modern conveniences can be found throughout the design including a utility room with a sink, lots of storage and counterspace perfect for organizing household chores. Plus, with the addition of the future space above the garage, this plan has an additional 336 square feet of living area perfect for a growing family.

Price Code E

Plan #587-007D-0030

Total Square Feet - 1,140

Bedrooms - 3

Baths - 2

Garage - 2-car drive under

Foundation - Basement

The welcoming front porch opens to the spacious living and dining areas that combine for easy family gatherings. An impressive organized kitchen has an abundance of cabinetry and a built-in pantry. Three bedrooms create a delightful family home.

Price Code AA

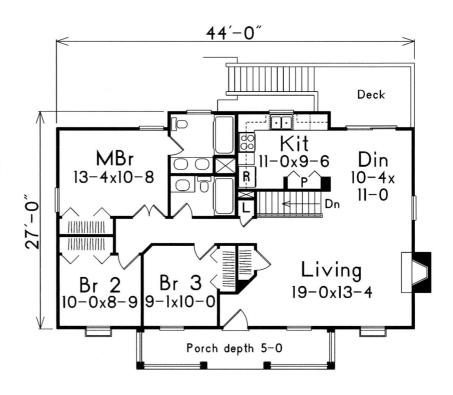

44'-0"

27'-0"

Deck

MBr
13-4x10-8

Kit
11-0x9-6

Din
10-4x
11-0

Br 2
10-0x8-9

Br 3
9-1x10-0

Living
19-0x13-4

Porch depth 5-0

Plan #587-001D-0040

Total Square Feet - 864

Bedrooms - 2

Baths - 1

Foundation - Crawl space, drawings also include basement and slab

An ideal starter or vacation home, this cottage is a charming retreat. The L-shaped kitchen with a convenient pantry serves the adjacent dining area with ease. Organization is an easy task with ample closet space in the bedrooms and coat, linen and laundry closets.

Price Code AAA

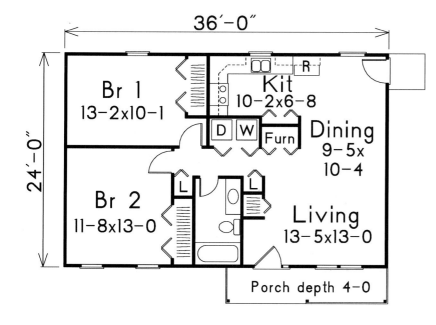

Plan #587-058D-0020

Total Square Feet - 1,428

Bedrooms - 3
Baths - 2
Foundation - Basement

The massive wrap-around porch
welcomes guests while offering an
abundance of outdoor living space.
The large vaulted family room opens
to the dining area and kitchen with
breakfast bar. The first floor master
bedroom offers a large bath, walk-in
closet and nearby laundry facilities.
On the second floor a spacious
loft/bedroom #3 overlooks the
family room and an additional
bedroom and bath round out this
enchanting cottage.

Price Code A

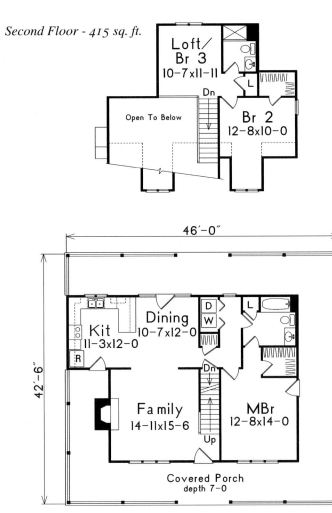

Second Floor - 415 sq. ft.

Loft/
Br 3
10-7x11-11

Open To Below

Dn

Br 2
12-8x10-0

46'-0"

42'-6"

Kit
11-3x12-0

Dining
10-7x12-0

D
W

L

Dn

Family
14-11x15-6

MBr
12-8x14-0

Up

Covered Porch
depth 7-0

First Floor - 1,013 sq. ft.

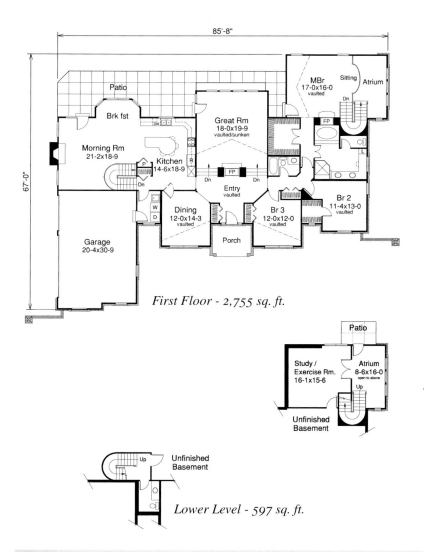

85'-8"

67'-0"

Patio

Brk fst

Morning Rm
21-2x18-9

Kitchen
14-6x18-9

Great Rm
18-0x19-9
vaulted/sunken

MBr
17-0x16-0
vaulted

Sitting

Atrium

FP

Entry
vaulted

FP

Br 2
11-4x13-0
vaulted

Dining
12-0x14-3
vaulted

Porch

Br 3
12-0x12-0
vaulted

Garage
20-4x30-9

W
D

First Floor - 2,755 sq. ft.

Patio

Study /
Exercise Rm.
16-1x15-6

Atrium
8-6x16-0
open to above

Up

Unfinished
Basement

Up   Unfinished
Basement

Lower Level - 597 sq. ft.

Plan #587-007D-0165

Total Square Feet - 3,352

Bedrooms - 3
Baths - 2 1/2
Garage -3-car side entry
Foundation - Walk-out basement

A see-through fireplace is the focal point of the spacious vaulted entry and grand sunken great room. An awesome private place for family gatherings is created by the luxurious kitchen, bayed breakfast area and morning room with fireplace. Secluded at the rear of the home, the master bedroom features a vaulted ceiling, open atrium with two-story arched window wall, balcony for sitting and a posh bath that shares a see-through fireplace. A private stairway leads down to the lower level which houses a study/exercise room.

Price Code F

Plan #587-040D-0027

Total Square Feet - 1,597

Bedrooms - 4

Baths - 2 1/2

Garage - 2-car detached

Foundation - Basement

The spacious family room offers a grand first impression of the home and includes a fireplace and coat closet. Nearby the open kitchen and dining room provide a breakfast bar and access to the outdoors. Convenient laundry area is tucked near the kitchen and has a side entrance into the home. The secluded master bedroom enjoys a walk-in closet and private bath, while the secondary bedrooms are housed on the second floor and share a full bath.

Price Code C

Second Floor - 615 sq. ft.

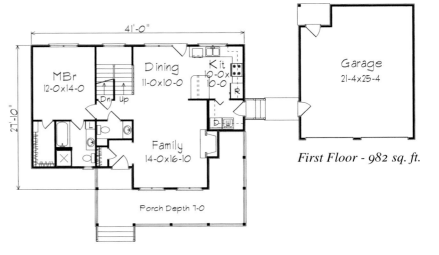

First Floor - 982 sq. ft.

Total Square Feet - 2,076
Bedrooms - 3
Baths - 2
Garage - 2-car
Foundation - Basement

This stunning ranch home captivates audiences with elegant features throughout. Directly off the foyer a study provides a great location for a home office. The vaulted great room boasts a fireplace flanked by windows and skylights that welcome the sun. Nearby, the kitchen leads to the vaulted breakfast room and rear deck, extending the dining opportunities to the outdoors. Large bay windows grace the master bedroom and bath bringing in calming light.

Price Code C

Plan #587-040D-0001

Total Square Feet - 1,833

Bedrooms - 3

Baths - 2 1/2

Garage - 2-car detached side entry

Foundation - Crawl space, drawings also include slab

A large porch greets guests and leads them into the family room warmed by a grand fireplace. The spacious dining area is brightened by large windows and patio access. The large, private master bedroom includes a spacious bath with garden tub, separate shower and large walk-in closet. A detached two-car garage with walkway leading to the house adds charm to this country home.

Price Code D

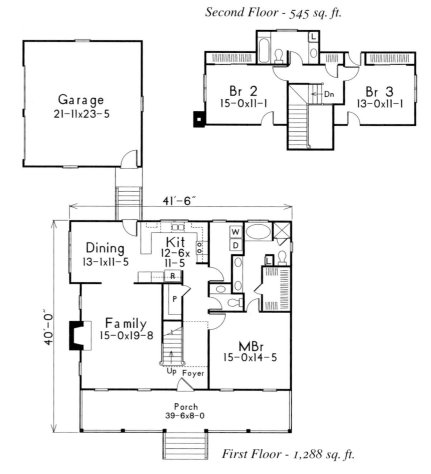

Second Floor - 545 sq. ft.

Br 2
15-0x11-1

Br 3
13-0x11-1

Garage
21-11x23-5

41'-6"

40'-0"

Dining
13-1x11-5

Kit
12-6x
11-5

W
D

Family
15-0x19-8

MBr
15-0x14-5

Up Foyer

Porch
39-6x8-0

First Floor - 1,288 sq. ft.

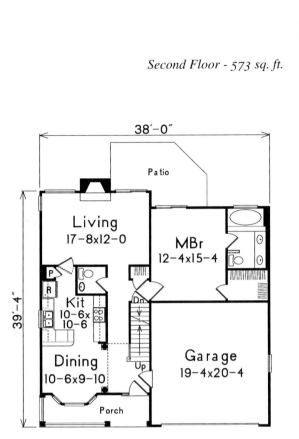

Second Floor - 573 sq. ft.

Br 2
17-8x12-0

Dn

Br 3
10-6x13-0

open to below

L

38'-0"

Patio

39'-4"

Living
17-8x12-0

MBr
12-4x15-4

P
R

Kit
10-6x 10-6

Dn

Dining
10-6x9-10

Up

Garage
19-4x20-4

Porch

First Floor - 951 sq. ft.

Total Square Feet - 1,524

Bedrooms - 3
Baths - 2 1/2
Garage - 2-car

Foundation - Basement, drawings
also include crawl space and slab

*Bayed dining room is charming and
bright and adds character to the
facade. Roomy first floor master
bedroom offers quiet privacy. The
second floor offers two secondary
bedrooms with walk-in closets, a
full bath and a delightful balcony
overlooking the two-story entry
illuminated by an oval window.*

Price Code B

Plan #587-040D-0007

Total Square Feet - 2,073

Bedrooms - 4

Baths - 2 1/2

Garage - 2-car side entry

Foundation - Basement

Box window decorates facade and creates a warm ambiance in the formal dining room. The family room provides an ideal gathering area with a fireplace, large windows and vaulted ceiling. The kitchen features an angled bar connecting it to the breakfast area for maximum efficiency. Private first floor master bedroom pampers the homeowners with a vaulted ceiling and luxury bath. On the second floor, the secondary bedrooms enjoy an abundance of closet space and share a compartmented bath.

Price Code D

Second Floor - 632 sq. ft.

First Floor - 1,441 sq. ft.

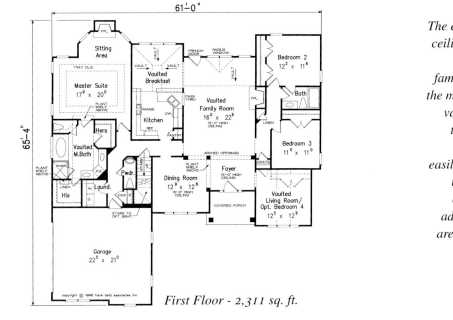

Optional Second Floor - 425 sq. ft.

First Floor - 2,311 sq. ft.

Total Square Feet - 2,311

Bedrooms - 3

Baths - 2 1/2

Garage - 2-car side entry

Foundation - Walk-out basement, slab or crawl space, please specify when ordering

The elegant foyer is topped with a 15' ceiling and features arched openings into the dining room and vaulted family room. Grand fireplaces warm the master suite and family room. The vaulted breakfast room is adjacent to the kitchen with a handy snack bar. The formal living room can easily be made into a fourth bedroom if needed. On the second floor an optional bonus room provides an additional 425 square feet of living area with a walk-in closet and bath.

Price Code D

Plan #587-007D-0102

Total Square Feet - 1,452

Bedrooms - 4

Baths - 2

Foundation - Basement

This grand design will fit any narrow lot and does not skimp on style. Enter at the large living room which features a cozy corner fireplace, bayed dining area and coat closet. The forward master bedroom enjoys having its own bath and linen closet. Three additional bedrooms share a bath with a double-bowl vanity to make sharing a simple task.

Price Code A

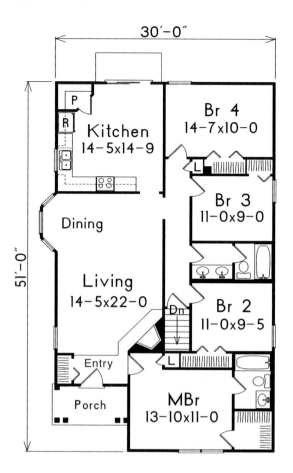

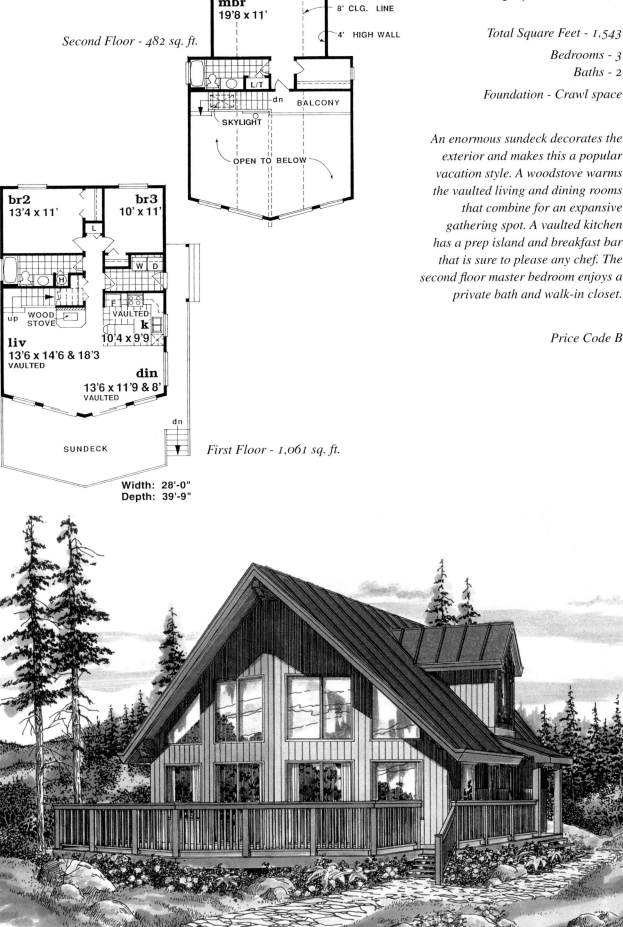

Plan #587-062D-0048

Second Floor - 482 sq. ft.

mbr
19'8 x 11'

8' CLG. LINE
4' HIGH WALL

L/T

dn   BALCONY

SKYLIGHT

OPEN TO BELOW

Total Square Feet - 1,543

Bedrooms - 3

Baths - 2

Foundation - Crawl space

An enormous sundeck decorates the exterior and makes this a popular vacation style. A woodstove warms the vaulted living and dining rooms that combine for an expansive gathering spot. A vaulted kitchen has a prep island and breakfast bar that is sure to please any chef. The second floor master bedroom enjoys a private bath and walk-in closet.

Price Code B

br2
13'4 x 11'

br3
10' x 11'

L

W   D

H

F

VAULTED

up

WOOD
STOVE

k
10'4 x 9'9

liv
13'6 x 14'6 & 18'3
VAULTED

din
13'6 x 11'9 & 8'
VAULTED

dn

SUNDECK

First Floor - 1,061 sq. ft.

Width: 28'-0"
Depth: 39'-9"

Plan #587-027D-0007

Total Square Feet - 2,444

Bedrooms - 3

Baths - 2 1/2

Garage - 2-car side entry

Foundation - Basement

The breathtaking entry leads to the great room defined by decorative columns. The kitchen enjoys a cooktop island and easy access to the formal dining room and bayed breakfast area. A laundry room with workspace, pantry and coat closet is adjacent to the kitchen. A large walk-in closet and private bath make this master bedroom one you're sure to enjoy. Two bedrooms, a study, full bath and plenty of closets are on the second floor. An abundance of windows throughout the entire home make this a cheerful and warm environment.

Price Code D

Second Floor - 772 sq. ft.

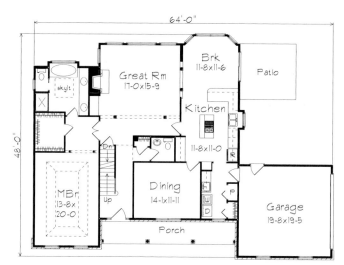

First Floor - 1,672 sq. ft.

Total Square Feet - 2,808
Bedrooms - 3
Baths - 2 1/2
Garage - 3-car side entry
Foundation - Basement

An impressive front exterior showcases three porches for quiet times. Once inside, view the large living and dining rooms that flank the elegant entry. Bedroom #3 shares a porch with the living room and a spacious bath with bedroom #2. On the opposite side of the home, the vaulted master bedroom enjoys a secluded screened porch and sumptuous bath with corner tub, double vanities and huge walk-in closet. For flexibility the living room can easily convert to an optional fourth bedroom.

Price Code F

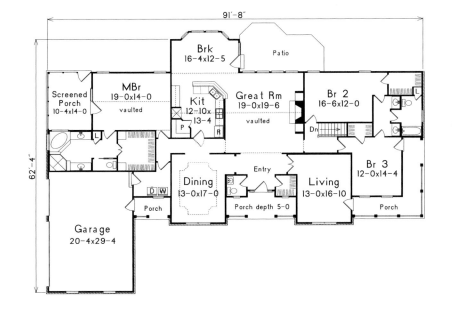

Plan #587-028D-0004

Total Square Feet - 1,785

Bedrooms - 3
Baths - 3
Garage - 2-car detached

Foundation - Basement, crawl space
or slab, please specify when ordering

For added spaciousness, 9' ceilings
top rooms throughout the home. A
luxurious master bath includes a
whirlpool tub and separate shower.
The cozy breakfast area is convenient
to the kitchen and the perfect place
to start your day.

Price Code B

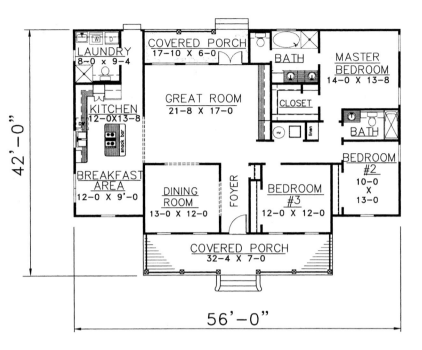

Total Square Feet - 1,992

Bedrooms - 3
Baths - 2 1/2
Garage - 3-car side entry
*Foundation - Basement, crawl space
or slab, please specify when ordering*

*Upon entering this amazing ranch,
you will view the breathtaking
formal dining and spacious family
rooms topped with 10' ceilings. The
bayed breakfast room overlooks
the outdoor deck and connects to
the screened porch extending the
dining opportunities to the outdoors.
A private formal living room in
the front of the home could easily
be converted to a home office or
study. Three private bedrooms and
an efficient kitchen round out this
delightful family home.*

Price Code C

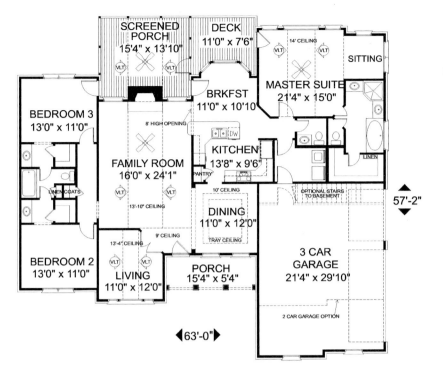

Plan #587-007D-0085

Total Square Feet - 1,787

Bedrooms - 3
Baths - 2
Garage - 2-car drive under
Foundation - Walk-out basement

The large great room is stunning
with a fireplace, vaulted ceiling,
three skylights and windows galore.
Cooking is sure to be a pleasure in
this L-shaped well-appointed kitchen
which includes a bayed breakfast
area with access to the rear deck.
Every bedroom offers a spacious
walk-in closet with a convenient
laundry room just steps away. An
optional lower level can be finished
as needed and provides 415 square
feet of living area.

Price Code B

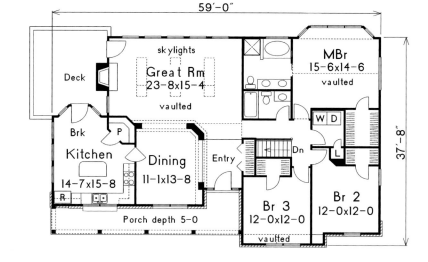

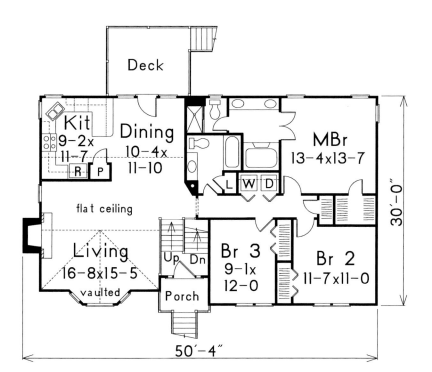

Total Square Feet - 1,404

Bedrooms - 3

Baths - 2

Garage - 2-car drive under

*Foundation - Basement, drawings
also include partial crawl space*

*A split-foyer entrance greets guests.
The bayed living area features a
unique vaulted ceiling and fireplace.
Nearby, the wrap-around kitchen has
corner windows for added sunlight
and a bar that overlooks the dining
area. A handy rear deck extends the
dining opportunities to the outdoors.
Tucked away for privacy, the relaxing
master bath features a garden tub
with separate shower.*

Price Code A

Plan #587-007D-0062

Total Square Feet - 2,483

Bedrooms - 4

Baths - 2

Garage - 2-car side entry

Foundation - Basement

Conveniences abound in this stunning ranch home. A large entry porch with open brick arches and a palladian door welcomes guests. The vaulted great room features an entertainment center alcove and the ideal layout for furniture placement. The dining room is extra large with a stylish tray ceiling, providing an elegant setting for formal entertaining. A convenient kitchen with wrap-around counter, menu desk and pantry opens to the cozy breakfast area.

Price Code D

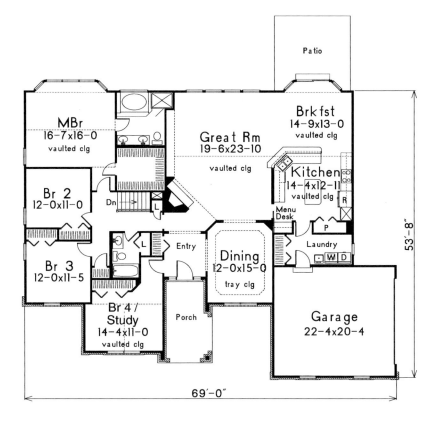

Total Square Feet - 2,396

Bedrooms - 4

Baths - 2

Garage - 2-car

Foundation - Slab, drawings also include basement and crawl space

Designed with style and beauty from the inside out, this home is also designed to be energy efficient with 2" x 6" exterior walls perfect for maintaining economical heating and cooling costs year-round. A generously wide entry welcomes guests. The central living area with a 12' ceiling and large fireplace serves as a convenient traffic hub. The efficient kitchen is secluded, yet has easy access to the living, dining and breakfast areas. The deluxe master bath has a walk-in closet, oversized tub, shower and other amenities to pamper the homeowners.

Price Code D

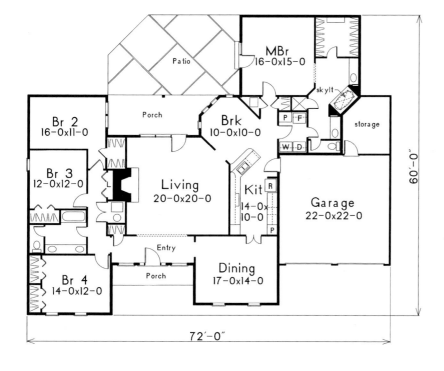

Plan #587-006D-0003

Total Square Feet - 1,674

Bedrooms - 3
Baths - 2
Garage - 2-car

Foundation - Basement, drawings
also include crawl space and slab

Delightful ranch has all the amenities
at an affordable cost. The vaulted
great room, dining area and kitchen
all enjoy a central fireplace and log
bin. A convenient laundry/mud room
is located between the garage and
the rest of the home with handy stairs
to the basement. Easily expandable
screened porch and adjacent patio
access the dining area, extending
meals to the outdoors. The relaxing
master bedroom features a full bath
with tub, separate shower and walk-
in closet. Two secondary bedrooms,
with full bath and linen closet nearby
round out this home designed with
family in mind.

Price Code B

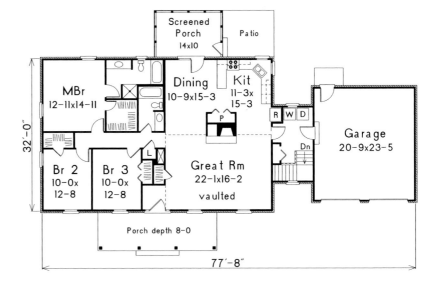

55'-8"

Balcony

MBr
18-4x13-0

Kit
10-2x
11-9

Dining | Dn

Great Rm
16-0x21-4
vaulted

46'-4"

W D

Entry

Porch depth 6-0

Br 2
12-8x14-0

Br 3
11-4x12-6

First Floor - 1,684 sq. ft.

Up

Garage
22-4x26-8

Family
15-6x20-8

Unfinished

Optional Lower Level - 611 sq. ft.

Plan #587-007D-0075

Total Square Feet - 1,684

Bedrooms - 3

Baths - 2

Garage - 2-car drive under

Foundation - Walk-out basement

Delightful wrap-around porch is
anchored by a full masonry fireplace.
The vaulted great room includes a
large bay window, fireplace, dining
balcony and atrium window wall.
Double walk-in closets, a large
luxury bath and sliding doors to an
exterior balcony are a few fantastic
features of the master bedroom. The
cheerful atrium opens to 611 square
feet of optional living area on the
lower level including a family room
and storage closet.

Price Code B

Rear View

Plan #587-001D-0086

Total Square Feet - 1,154

Bedrooms - 3
Baths - 1 1/2
Foundation - Crawl space, drawings
also include slab

Escape from stress in this enchanting
vacation retreat. A large front deck
opens into the enormous living/dining
room. The U-shaped kitchen features
a large breakfast bar keeping the
area open and a handy laundry area.
Bedroom #1 on the first floor enjoys
a large closet and nearby full bath
making it ideal as the master suite.
Private second floor bedrooms share
a half bath.

Price Code AA

Second Floor - 434 sq. ft.

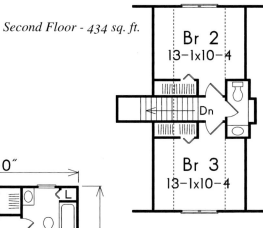

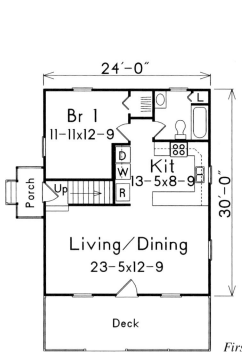

First Floor - 720 sq. ft.

Second Floor - 1,746 sq. ft.

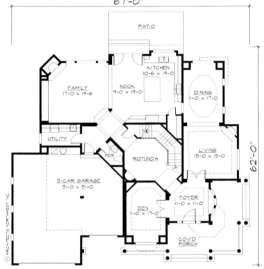

67'-0"

62'-0"

First Floor - 2,000 sq. ft.

Plan #587-071D-0006

Total Square Feet - 3,746

Bedrooms - 4

Baths - 3 1/2

Garage - 3-car

Foundation - Crawl space

Upon entering the large foyer guests are greeted by a beautiful central two-story rotunda with an angled staircase. An oval tray ceiling in the formal dining room creates a Victorian feel. The two-story family room is sunny and bright with windows on two floors. Spacious bedrooms create the ultimate family home. The second floor bonus room is the perfect spot for a game room and has an additional 314 square feet of living area. Live in luxury with this one-of-a-kind home plan.

Price Code G

Plan #587-028D-0008

Total Square Feet - 2,156

Bedrooms - 4

Baths - 3

Garage - 2-car side entry

Foundation - Basement, crawl space
or slab, please specify when ordering

Pampering elements make this the
perfect place to come home to. The
secluded master bedroom has a spa-
style bath with a corner whirlpool
tub, large shower, double sinks and
a walk-in closet. All these features
create a sense of sheer elegance and
ease when getting ready to begin
your day. Throughout this home,
plenty of windows add an open, airy
feel especially in the great room and
breakfast room which both enjoy
pleasant views to the rear patio.

Price Code C

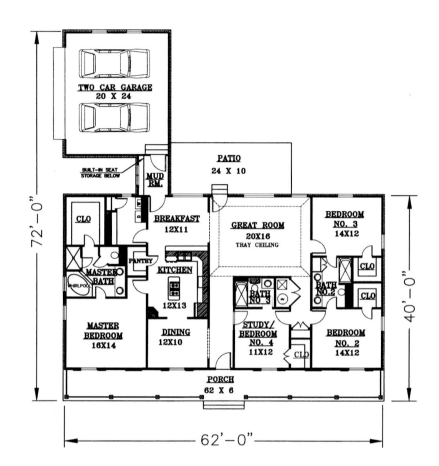

Total Square Feet - 1,795

Bedrooms - 3

Baths - 2 1/2

Foundation - Basement or crawl space, please specify when ordering

Build a private vacation retreat with an abundance of windows, large deck and sunken spa tub. The window wall in the combined living and dining areas brings the outdoors in. The first floor master bedroom has a full bath and walk-in closet. Vaulted loft on the second floor is a unique feature and has room for a small play area or computer center.

Price Code B

Second Floor - 638 sq. ft.

First Floor - 1,157 sq. ft.

Width: 36'-0"
Depth: 40'-0"

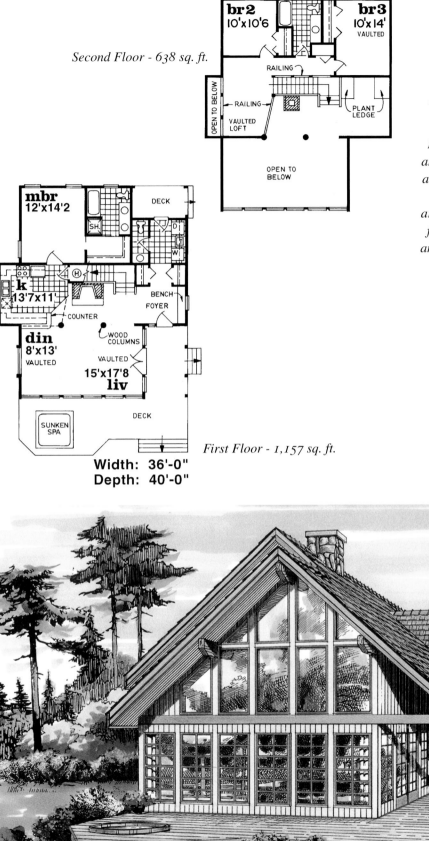

Plan #587-011D-0046

Total Square Feet - 2,277

Bedrooms - 4

Baths - 3

Garage - 2-car

Foundation - Crawl space

The foyer spills into the open living area. Lots of windows in the great room create an inviting feeling. An enormous dining area and kitchen combine to create a large gathering area overlooking into the great room. First floor den/bedroom #4 would make an ideal home office, offering flexibility with this plan. The bedrooms are located on the second floor for peace and quiet.

Price Code E

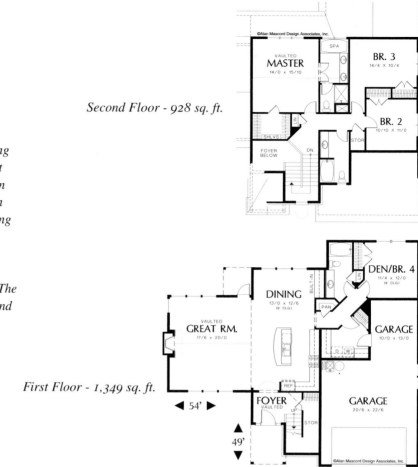

Second Floor - 928 sq. ft.

First Floor - 1,349 sq. ft.

Second Floor - 855 sq. ft.

Total Square Feet - 2,597

Bedrooms - 4
Baths - 3 1/2
Garage - 2-car side entry

Foundation - Walk-out basement, drawings also include crawl space and slab

Brick and arched windows create a radiant exterior while the interior is filled with spectacular features. The entry and great room are enhanced by a sweeping balcony above and a vaulted ceiling and transomed arch windows. A large U-shaped kitchen features an island cooktop and breakfast bar. On the second floor, bedrooms #2 and #3 share a bath, while bedroom #4 has a private bath.

Price Code E

First Floor - 1,742 sq. ft.

Plan #587-028D-0001

Total Square Feet - 864

Bedrooms - 2

Baths - 1

Foundation - Crawl space or slab, please specify when ordering

This adorable waterfront cottage is sure to capture hearts. A spacious living/dining room greets those who enter and a snack bar in the kitchen keeps the area open while creating a quick and easy meal area. The large laundry area accesses the outdoors as well as the kitchen and offers convenience that is hard to find in small homes.

Price Code AAA

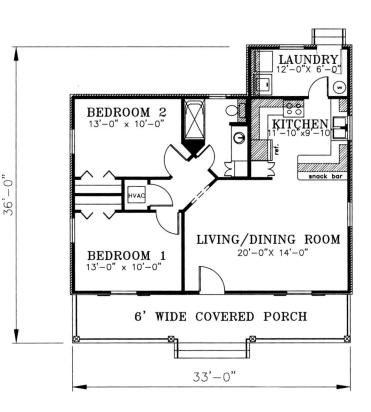

LAUNDRY
12'-0" X 6'-0"

BEDROOM 2
13'-0" x 10'-0"

KITCHEN
11'-10"x9'-10"

ref.

snack bar

HVAC

BEDROOM 1
13'-0" x 10'-0"

LIVING/DINING ROOM
20'-0"X 14'-0"

6' WIDE COVERED PORCH

36'-0"

33'-0"

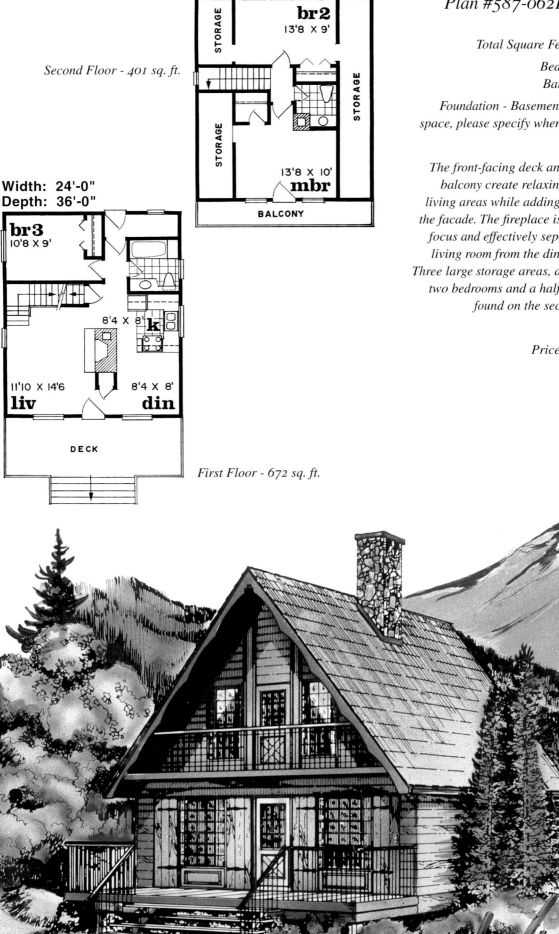

Plan #587-062D-0031

Second Floor - 401 sq. ft.

br2
13'8 X 9'

STORAGE

STORAGE

STORAGE

13'8 X 10'
mbr

BALCONY

Width: 24'-0"
Depth: 36'-0"

br3
10'8 X 9'

8'4 X 8' **k**

11'10 X 14'6

8'4 X 8'

liv   **din**

DECK

First Floor - 672 sq. ft.

Total Square Feet - 1,073

Bedrooms - 3
Baths - 1 1/2

Foundation - Basement or crawl
space, please specify when ordering

The front-facing deck and covered
balcony create relaxing outdoor
living areas while adding charm to
the facade. The fireplace is the main
focus and effectively separates the
living room from the dining room.
Three large storage areas, along with
two bedrooms and a half bath, are
found on the second floor.

Price Code AA

Plan #587-007D-0050

Total Square Feet - 2,723

Bedrooms - 4
Baths - 2 1/2
Garage - 3-car side entry
Foundation - Basement

A large porch invites you into the
elegant foyer which accesses a
vaulted study with private hall and
coat closet. The great room is second
to none, comprised of a fireplace,
built-in shelves, a vaulted ceiling
and a 1 1/2 story window wall. A
spectacular hearth room with vaulted
ceiling and masonry fireplace opens
to an elaborate kitchen featuring two
snack bars, a cooking island and
walk-in pantry. Three bedrooms and
an optional bedroom/study remain
private on the left side of the home
and provide room for family living.

Price Code E

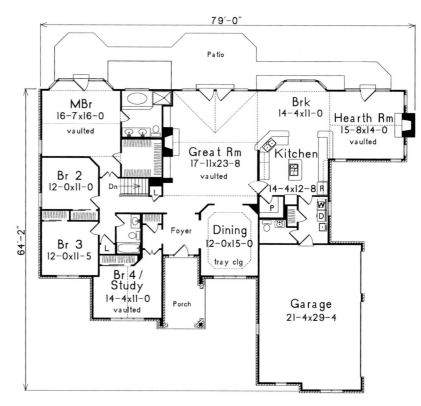

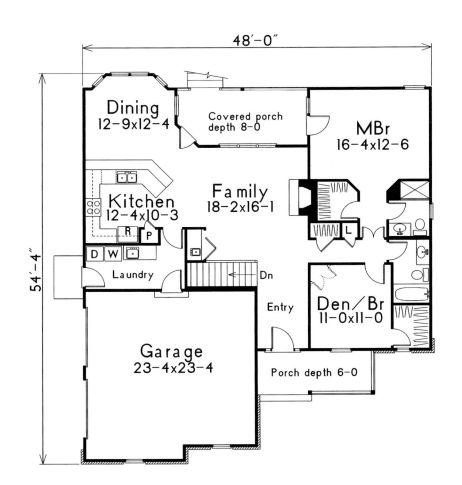

Total Square Feet - 1,440

Bedrooms - 2

Baths - 2

Garage - 2-car side entry

Foundation - Basement

This open floor plan showcases the generous family room with grand fireplace and wet bar. The well-designed kitchen offers a handy snack bar that opens to the cozy bayed dining room. The laundry/mud room between the kitchen and garage is a convenient feature. Lots of linen, pantry and closet space throughout keeps everyone organized.

Price Code A

Plan #587-038D-0040

Total Square Feet - 1,642

Bedrooms - 3
Baths - 2
Garage - 2-car
Foundation - Crawl space

Grace and charm welcome guests. A formal dining room with built-in cabinet and intimate parlor flank the entry showcasing the Traditional style of the ranch. The secluded master bedroom includes a private bath with dressing table. The secondary bedrooms are on the opposite side of the home and share an oversized bath.

Price Code B

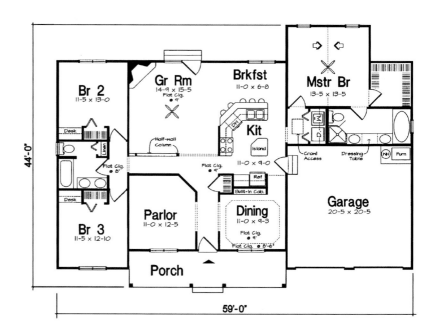

Total Square Feet - 676

Bedrooms - 1

Baths - 1

Foundation - Crawl space

Cozy cottage is perfect for weekend getaways. The full-length front covered porch is perfect for enjoying the outdoors. A see-through fireplace between the bedroom and living area adds character and warmth. Combined dining and living areas create an open feeling. With additional storage available in the utility room, this home has plenty of space.

Price Code AAA

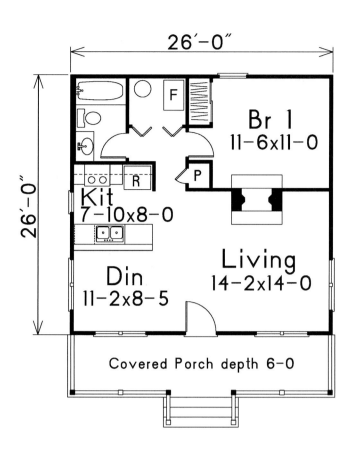

26'-0"

26'-0"

Br 1
11-6x11-0

Kit
7-10x8-0

Din
11-2x8-5

Living
14-2x14-0

F

R

P

Covered Porch depth 6-0

Plan #587-007D-0065

Total Square Feet - 2,218

Bedrooms - 4

Baths - 2

Garage - 2-car

Foundation - Walk-out basement

Upon entering, view the vaulted great room with arched colonnade entry, bay windowed atrium with staircase and a fireplace. The large kitchen enjoys a pass-through breakfast bar and walk-in pantry. Nearby, the breakfast room offers a bay window and access onto the rear deck. The majestic atrium opens to 1,217 square feet of optional living area below including a family room with fireplace, wet bar, full bath and two bedrooms.

Price Code D

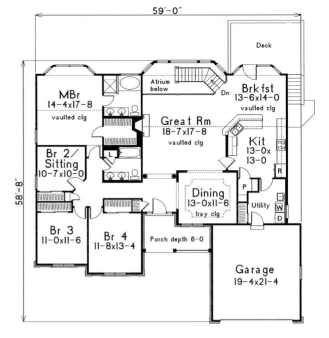

First Floor - 2,218 sq. ft.

Optional Lower Level - 1,217 sq. ft.

Rear View

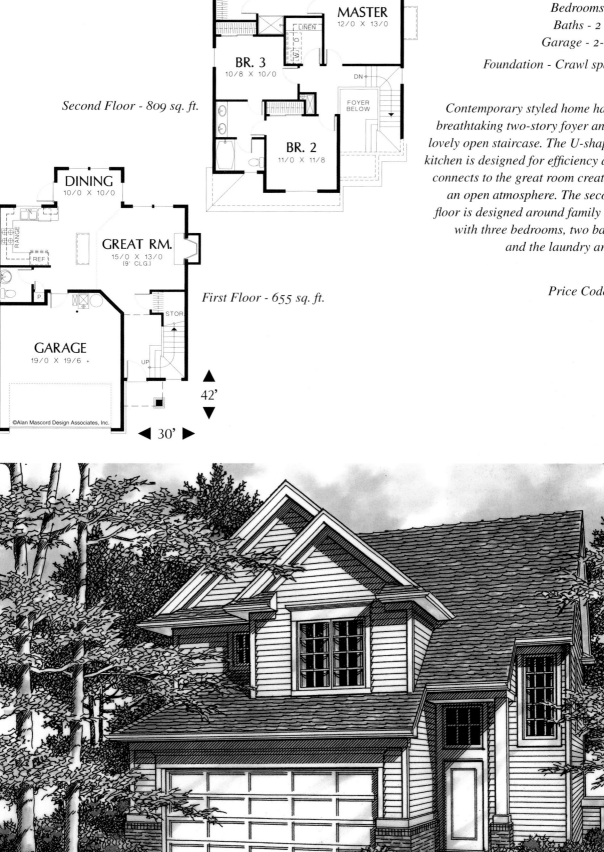

Second Floor - 809 sq. ft.

MASTER
12/0 X 13/0

LINEN

BR. 3
10/8 X 10/0

W D

DN

FOYER
BELOW

BR. 2
11/0 X 11/8

DINING
10/0 X 10/0

RANGE

REF

GREAT RM.
15/0 X 13/0
(9' CLG.)

First Floor - 655 sq. ft.

P

STOR

GARAGE
19/0 X 19/6 +

UP

©Alan Mascord Design Associates, Inc.

42'

30'

Total Square Feet - 1,464
Bedrooms - 3
Baths - 2 1/2
Garage - 2-car
Foundation - Crawl space

Contemporary styled home has a
breathtaking two-story foyer and a
lovely open staircase. The U-shaped
kitchen is designed for efficiency and
connects to the great room creating
an open atmosphere. The second
floor is designed around family life
with three bedrooms, two baths
and the laundry area.

Price Code C

Plan #587-035D-0011

Total Square Feet - 1,945

Bedrooms - 4

Baths - 2

Garage - 2-car side entry

Foundation - Walk-out basement, crawl space or slab, please specify when ordering

Elegant dining room has an arched window that also adds character to the exterior. The vaulted breakfast room is directly off the great room with a plant shelf above and enjoys a French door to the rear patio. The master suite is separate from other bedrooms for privacy and pampers the homeowners with a deluxe bath.

Price Code C

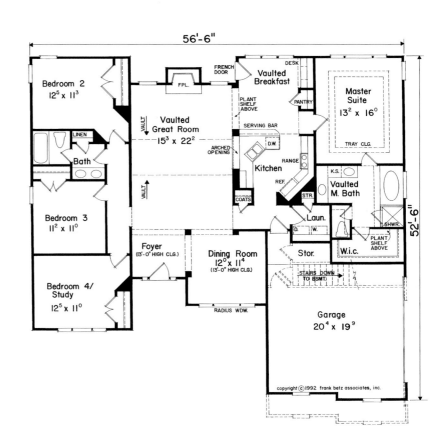

Second Floor - 1,544 sq. ft.

Br 5
12-1x14-3

Sunken Solarium Below

Br 2
13-11x15-9

Loft

Dn

Br 4
12-1x12-0

Library
15-8x9-8

Br 3
15-5x12-0

open to below

Total Square Feet - 3,850
Bedrooms - 5
Baths - 3 1/2
Garage - 3-car
Foundation - Basement

A gorgeous entry, with balcony above, leads into a splendid great room with sunken solarium. Upon entering the solarium one will find a space featuring U-shaped stairs with a balcony and an arched window. Pass through the cozy hearth room into the kitchen designed with a half-circle bar and cooktop island with banquet-sized dining nearby. In addition, the master bedroom includes a luxurious bath and large study with a cheerful bay window.

Price Code F

80'-8"

Patio

Brk

Hearth Rm
12-1x18-3

Sunken Solarium

Kit
13-10x18-0
vaulted

MBr
16-8x13-0

Dining
12-1x16-0

Great Rm
18-0x21-8

Study
16-8x12-3

Up Dn

51'-8"

Garage
30-4x21-4

Entry

First Floor - 2,306 sq. ft.

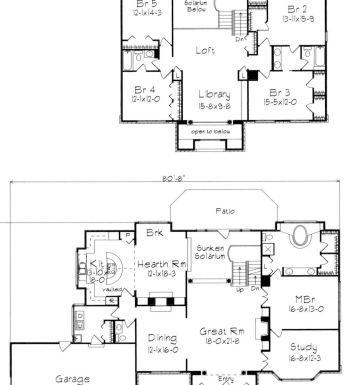

Interior View

Plan #587-058D-0012

Total Square Feet - 1,143

Bedrooms - 2

Baths - 1

Foundation - Crawl space

An appealing open feel has been created to make this home truly inviting in every way. The vaulted family room and kitchen create an open atmosphere. Placing an enormous stone fireplace in the family room adds warmth and character to all the gathering areas. Just beyond is a spacious kitchen with a breakfast bar overlooking the family room. This home also includes a separate dining area great for entertaining.

Price Code AA

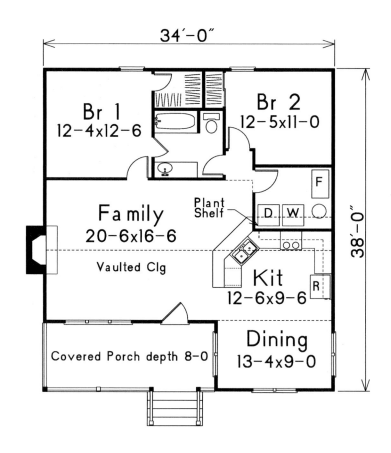

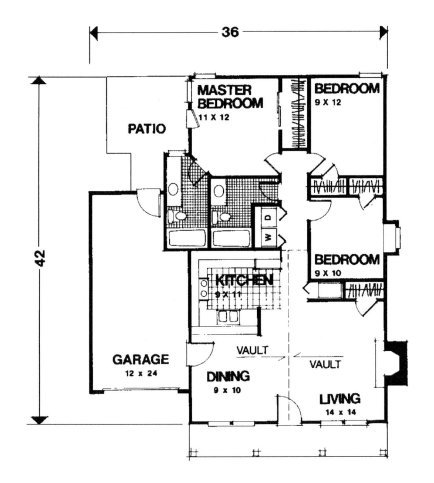

Total Square Feet - 1,050

Bedrooms - 3
Baths - 2
Garage - 1-car

Foundation - Basement or slab,
please specify when ordering

Vaulted ceilings in the living and dining areas create a feeling of spaciousness when entering this home. An efficient U-shaped kitchen provides the perfect amount of organization especially with a convenient laundry room near all of the bedrooms. In addition, the master bedroom has its own private bath and access to the outdoors onto a private patio

Price Code AA

Plan #587-001D-0007

Total Square Feet - 2,874

Bedrooms - 4
Baths - 2 1/2
Garage - 2-car side entry
Foundation - Basement

Enter the large foyer which opens
to the family room with a massive
stone fireplace and open stairs to
the basement and find a sloped
ceiling and wood beams adjoining
the kitchen and breakfast area with
windows on two walls. Plus, this
home has an ultra private master
bedroom including a raised tub under
the bay window, a dramatic dressing
area and a huge walk-in closet.

Price Code E

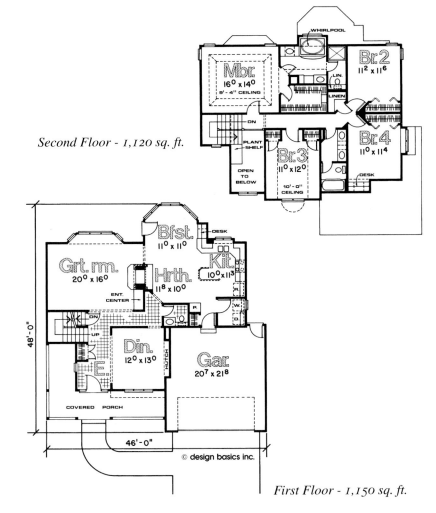

Second Floor - 1,120 sq. ft.

Total Square Feet - 2,270

Bedrooms - 4

Baths - 2 1/2

Garage - 2-car

Foundation - Basement

The first floor has a terrific floor plan for entertaining featuring a large kitchen, breakfast area and adjacent great room. Plus, the great room and hearth room share a see-through fireplace illuminating each room with warmth and light in a subtle and inviting way. Another terrific feature of this home are the oversized rooms throughout.

Price Code D

© design basics inc.

First Floor - 1,150 sq. ft.

Plan #587-058D-0021

Total Square Feet - 1,477

Bedrooms - 3
Baths - 2
Garage - 2-car side entry with storage area
Foundation - Basement

A deep oversized porch provides protection from the elements whatever the weather. A terrific area of this home is the kitchen which employs a step-saving design while also featuring a snack bar which opens to the breakfast room with bay window. Memorable family times will no doubt be enjoyed in the comfort of this home.

Price Code A

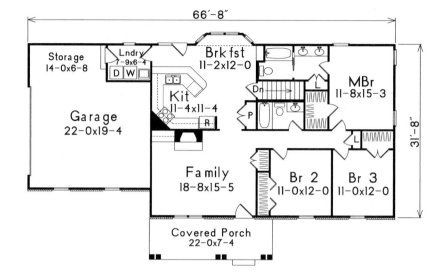

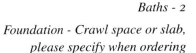

Plan #587-028D-0006

Total Square Feet - 1,700

Bedrooms - 3
Baths - 2

Foundation - Crawl space or slab,
please specify when ordering

A well-organized interior with plenty of storage will keep this home neat and tidy. The oversized laundry room containing a large pantry and storage area as well as access to the outdoors helps to achieve this. High function in the kitchen includes a raised snack bar perfect with extra seating for dining. When the day is over, escape to the master bedroom which is separated from other bedrooms for peace and quiet.

Price Code B

50—0 WIDE X 42—0 DEEP
(INCLUDING COVERED PORCH)

BEDROOM NO. 3
14—0 X 14—0

KITCHEN
10—2X14—0

DINING
11—10X14—0

FREEZER   W   D   WH

LAUNDRY
12—0X7—0

PANTRY   STORAGE

STOVE

RAISED SNACK BAR

REF

DW

HVAC

LINEN

BATH NO. 2

LINEN   LINEN   HALL

BEDROOM NO. 2
14—0 X 12—0

VENTLESS
GAS FIREPLACE

CLOSET

M.
BATH

GREAT ROOM
22—0 X 20—0

MASTER
BEDROOM
12—0 X 14—0

COVERED PORCH
22—4 X 8—0

Plan #587-048D-0004

Total Square Feet - 2,397

Bedrooms - 3
Baths - 2 1/2
Garage - 2-car
Foundation - Slab

A gracious covered entrance with a fountain leads to the double-door entry and foyer. Once inside, the interior is open and spacious with the kitchen featuring two pantries and opening into the breakfast and family rooms. Total luxury will be enjoyed in the master bath featuring a huge walk-in closet, electric clothes carousel, double-bowl vanity and corner tub all waiting to pamper those who enter.

Price Code E

Total Square Feet - 1,783

Bedrooms - 3

Baths - 2

Garage - 2-car

Foundation - Slab

A double-door entry leads into the grand foyer and family room with a volume ceiling adding a tremendous amount of spaciousness to this living space. Extra storage is appreciated with the addition of the walk-in pantry in the kitchen. Luxury continues to play a major role in the master bath featuring a step-down doorless shower, a huge vanity and a large walk-in closet.

Price Code B

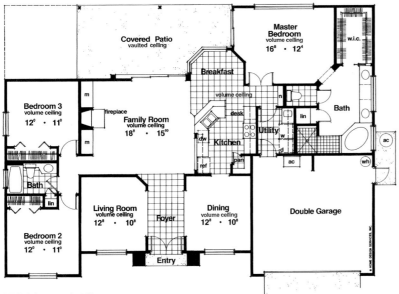

Width: 60'-0"
Depth: 45'-0"

Plan #587-021D-0012

Total Square Feet - 1,672

Bedrooms - 3
Baths - 2
Garage - 2-car side entry

Foundation - Crawl space, drawings also include basement and slab

Designed to be energy efficient, this home has 2" x 6" exterior walls and is loaded with curb appeal featuring covered front and rear porches. On the inside, 12' ceilings in the living room, kitchen and bedroom #2 add interest and spaciousness. The kitchen is complete with a pantry, an angled bar and adjacent eating area perfect for those casual meals. A sloped ceiling in the dining room adds character. Relax in the vaulted master bedroom which features a walk-in closet and adjoining bath with separate tub and shower.

Price Code C

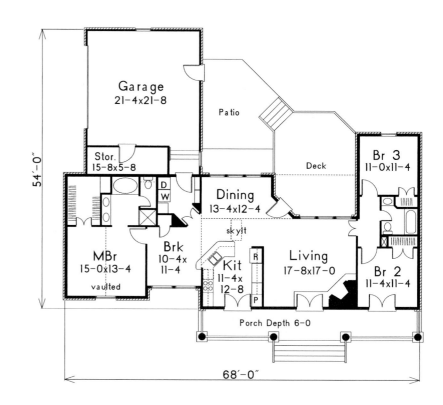

Total Square Feet - 1,850
Bedrooms - 3
Baths - 2
Garage - 2-car
Foundation - Basement

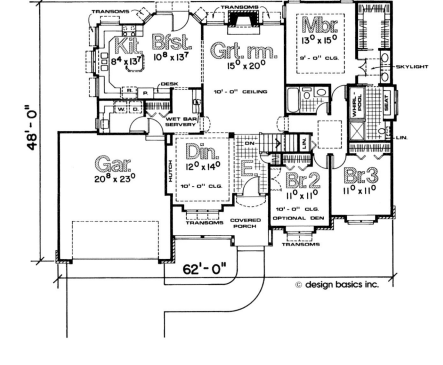

Oversized rooms throughout create a comfortable living environment for the entire family. The great room spotlights a fireplace with sunny windows on both sides. An interesting wet bar between the kitchen and dining area is an added bonus when entertaining family and friends. A unique skylighted bath in the master bedroom is the perfect place to enjoy some quiet time.

Price Code C

© design basics inc.

Plan #587-062D-0041

Total Square Feet - 1,541

Bedrooms - 3
Baths - 2
Garage - 2-car

Foundation - Basement or crawl
space, please specify when ordering

This rambling country style home
encourages outdoor enjoyment
thanks to the exceptional wrap-
around porch. Plus, the dining area
offers access to a screened
porch for outdoor dining and
entertaining. The large country
kitchen features a center island
and a breakfast bay for casual
meals bathed in sunlight.
A charming old-fashioned
woodstove is a nice touch
in the great room.

Price Code B

Width: 87'-0"
Depth: 39'-0"

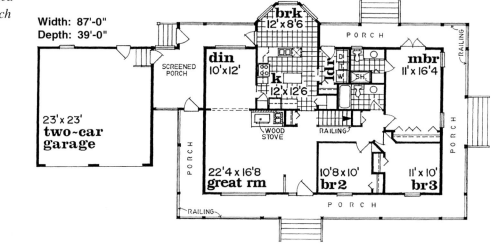

Total Square Feet - 1,609

Bedrooms - 4

Baths - 2

Garage - 2-car

Foundation - Basement

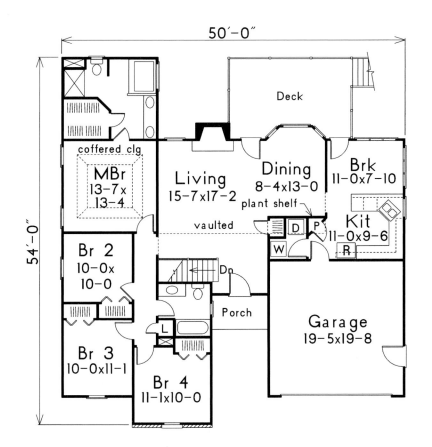

High style and efficiency reign in this plan. The kitchen includes a corner pantry and adjacent laundry room perfect for handling multiple chores. The breakfast room boasts plenty of windows and opens onto a rear deck for splendid outdoor dining. The front entry leads into a large living area with fireplace making an inviting first impression. Extra amenities are enjoyed by the master bedroom featuring a tray ceiling and private deluxe bath.

Price Code B

Plan #587-055D-0131

Total Square Feet - 1,461

Bedrooms - 3
Baths - 2
Garage - 2-car

Foundation - Slab, crawl space, basement or walk-out basement, please specify when ordering

Touches of elegance can be found throughout this home. The stunning great room has a 9' boxed ceiling and a handsome fireplace. The kitchen features a bar which is sure to see many quick meals and offer lots of convenience for busy families. The bayed dining room is full of natural light providing another terrific option when entertaining or more formal meals.

Price Code B

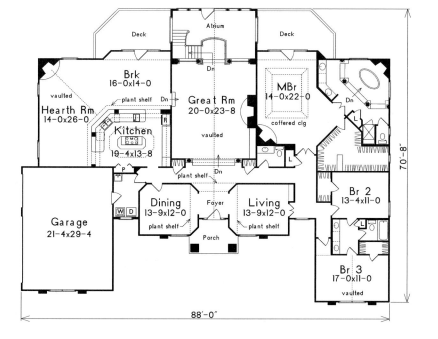

Total Square Feet - 3,814

Bedrooms - 3

Baths - 2 1/2

Garage - 3-car side entry

Foundation - Walk-out basement

This massive sunken great room with vaulted ceiling includes an exciting balcony overlook of a rear towering atrium window wall. This is just one of seven vaulted rooms adding drama to the interior of this home. Another unique amenity are the four fireplaces scattered throughout providing warmth and style around every corner. A large breakfast bar adjoins the open "California" kitchen. Don't forget the master bath complemented by the colonnade and fireplace surrounding the sunken tub and deck. Of the 3,814 square feet, 248 square feet is found in the lower level atrium.

Price Code G

Rear View

Plan #587-026D-0110

Total Square Feet - 1,999
Bedrooms - 4
Baths - 2 1/2
Garage - 2-car
Foundation - Basement

Combination breakfast room and kitchen create a spacious gathering place including access to the laundry area and a built-in desk area. Nearby, a private dining area with unique built-in hutch adds interest. In addition, the first floor master bedroom enjoys a private bath with a luxurious whirlpool tub perfect for tranquility.

Price Code C

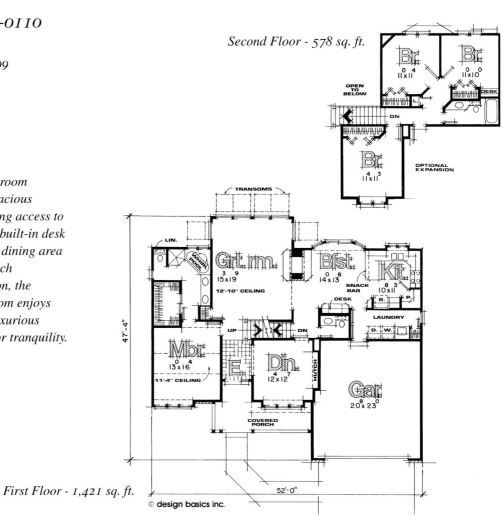

Second Floor - 578 sq. ft.

First Floor - 1,421 sq. ft.

© design basics inc.

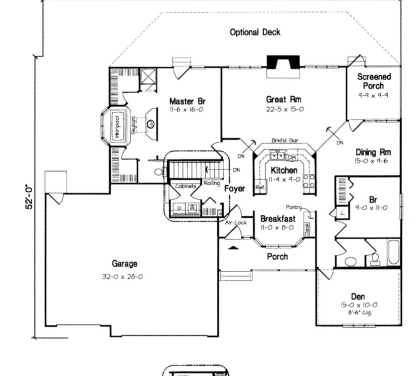

66'-0"

Optional Deck

Master Br
11-6 x 16-0

Great Rm
22-5 x 15-0

Screened
Porch
9-9 x 9-9

Whirlpool

Skylight

Brkfst Bar

DN

DN

Dining Rm
15-0 x 9-6

Kitchen
11-4 x 9-0

DW

Ref

Cabinets

Railing

Foyer

DN

Br
9-0 x 11-0

52'-0"

D

A

Air-Lock

Pantry

Breakfast
11-0 x 8-0

Desk

Garage
32-0 x 28-0

Porch

Den
15-0 x 10-0
8'-6" Clg.

Furn.

WH

Crawl
Space
Access

Crawl / Slab Option

Total Square Feet - 1,738

Bedrooms - 2

Baths - 2

Garage - 3-car

Foundation - Basement, crawl space or slab, please specify when ordering

Flexibility makes this home perfect for many families. A den in the front of the home can easily be converted to a third bedroom if needed. For added family or guests, the kitchen includes an eating nook. Step down into a large sunken great room centrally located with a cozy fireplace. Plus, the master bedroom has an unforgettable bath with a super skylight. Also, the detail to the left explains how the crawl space or slab foundation option works into the design.

Price Code B

Rear View

Plan #587-011D-0007

Total Square Feet - 1,580

Bedrooms - 3

Baths - 2 1/2

Garage - 2-car

Foundation - Crawl space

A covered porch off the rear of the home extends the great room to the outdoors. Built-in bookshelves flank one wall of the dining room and are perfect for collectibles or cookbooks and help make organizing fun and easy. A secluded master bedroom enjoys a vaulted ceiling, private bath with double vanity and a large walk-in closet.

Price Code C

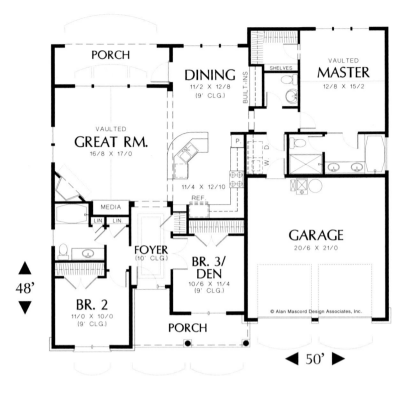

Total Square Feet - 2,097

Bedrooms - 3

Baths - 3

Garage - 3-car side entry

Foundation - Basement, crawl space or slab, please specify when ordering

Angles add interest in the country kitchen, family room and eating area. Plus, the family room includes a TV niche making this a cozy place to relax anytime. Or, if you prefer more privacy, relax in the sumptuous master bedroom including a sitting area, a double walk-in closet and a full bath with double vanities. Plus, this home provides a bonus room above the garage adding 452 square feet of additional living space if needed.

Price Code C

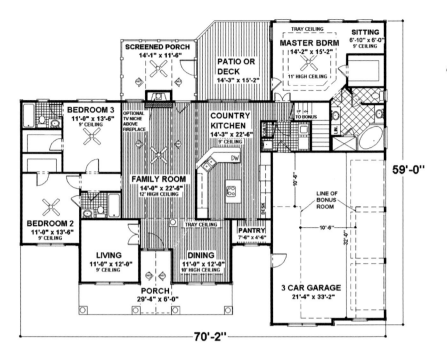

Plan #587-017D-0007

Total Square Feet - 1,567

Bedrooms - 3

Baths - 2

Garage - 2-car side entry

Foundation - Partial basement/crawl space, drawings also include slab

A gorgeous terrace across the rear of this home adds an elegant backdrop when eating in the breakfast area and cheerful, windowed dining area. The living room flows into the dining room shaped by an angled pass-through into the kitchen. Seclusion is enjoyed by the master bedroom which is separated from other bedrooms for privacy. A future area available on the second floor has an additional 338 square feet of living area perfect for a home office, children's play area or a casual family entertainment room.

Price Code C

Optional Second Floor - 338 sq. ft.

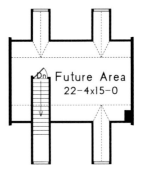

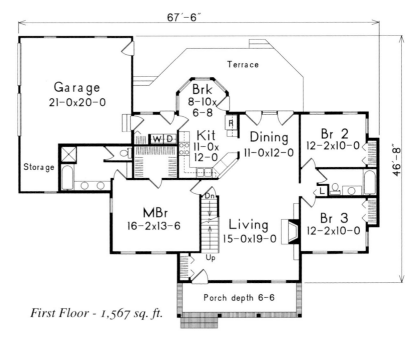

First Floor - 1,567 sq. ft.

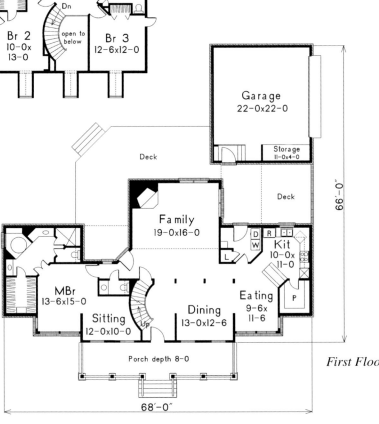

Second Floor - 595 sq. ft.

Total Square Feet - 2,360

Bedrooms - 3

Baths - 2 1/2

Garage - 2-car side entry

Foundation - Crawl space, drawings also include slab and basement

The curved staircase in the foyer will no doubt be an attention-getter upon entering this home. Beyond, the sloped family room ceiling provides a view from the second floor balcony. Efficiency is key in the kitchen featuring an island bar and walk-in butler's pantry. A sitting area and large bath help to create a pleasing and enjoyable master suite.

Price Code D

First Floor - 1,765 sq. ft.

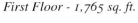

Plan #587-026D-0112

Total Square Feet - 1,911

Bedrooms - 3

Baths - 2

Garage - 2-car

Foundation - Basement

A large entry opens into a beautiful great room with an angled see-through fireplace enjoyed by the hearth and breakfast rooms as well. The terrific design features of this plan spill into the kitchen and breakfast area with an adjacent sunny bayed hearth room with a built-in entertainment center. Plus, the private master bedroom with bath features a skylight and walk-in closet.

Price Code C

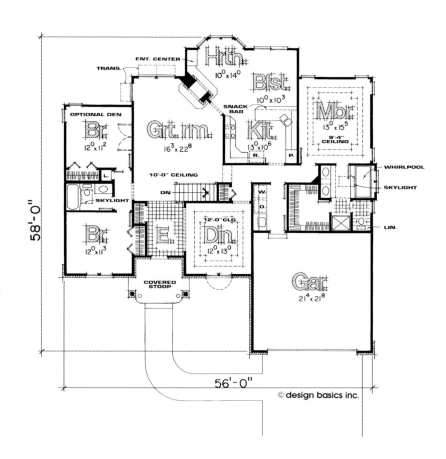

Total Square Feet - 2,597
Bedrooms - 4
Baths - 3
Garage - 3-car rear entry
Foundation - Slab

This angled design creates unlimited views and spaces that appear larger than their true size. A unique island kitchen with a view to the nook and family room includes a walk-in pantry. The highly functional pool bath is shared by outdoor and indoor areas making it a popular choice. Flexibility is available with the den/bedroom #4 which could make the perfect home office or guest suite depending on the need.

Price Code D

Width: 98'-6"
Depth: 50'-0"

Plan #587-011D-0047

Total Square Feet - 2,120

Bedrooms - 3

Baths - 2 1/2

Garage - 3-car

Foundation - Crawl space

An Arts and Crafts style prevails with the exterior of this design. Some terrific interior features include a first floor vaulted master bedroom with a spacious and open feel. Built-in shelves adorn the dining room creating a custom feel to the space. Plus, the office has a double-door entry helping to maintain privacy and quiet in an elegant and stylish way.

Price Code E

Second Floor - 517 sq. ft.

First Floor - 1,603 sq. ft.

Plan #587-038D-0039

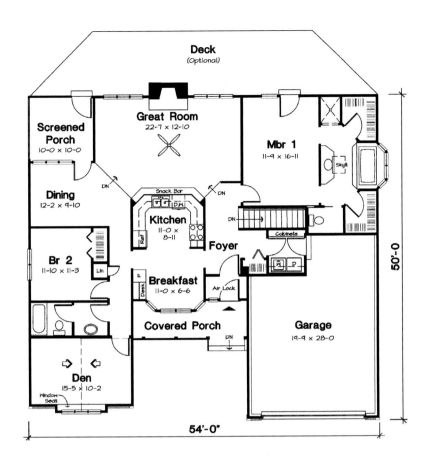

Deck
(Optional)

Great Room
22-7 x 12-10

Screened Porch
10-0 x 10-0

Mbr 1
11-9 x 16-11

Skylt

DN

Dining
12-2 x 9-10

Snack Bar

DN

DN

Kitchen
11-0 x 8-11

Ref

Foyer

DN

Cabinets

Br 2
11-10 x 11-3

Lin

Desk

Breakfast
11-0 x 6-6

Air Lock

Garage
19-9 x 28-0

Covered Porch

DN

Den
15-5 x 10-2

Window Seat

54'-0"

50'-0"

Total Square Feet - 1,771

Bedrooms - 2

Baths - 2

Garage - 2-car

Foundation - Basement, crawl space or slab foundation, please specify when ordering

This charming ranch definitely has something special inside and out. A central kitchen allows for convenient access when entertaining. The den has a sloped ceiling and charming window seat adding design and character to the interior. A very private master bedroom has access to the outdoors onto an expansive deck.

Price Code B

Plan #587-021D-0006

Total Square Feet - 1,600

Bedrooms - 3
Baths - 2
Garage - 2-car side entry
Foundation - Slab, drawings also
include crawl space and basement

An energy efficient home has been
created with the help of 2" x 6"
exterior walls. Upon entering, an
impressive sunken living room
features a massive stone fireplace
and 16' vaulted ceiling begging for
guests and family to relax and enjoy
the room. Nearby, the dining room
is conveniently located next to the
kitchen and divided for privacy.
Other special amenities include a
sewing room, glass shelves in the
kitchen, a grand master bath and a
large utility area.

Price Code C

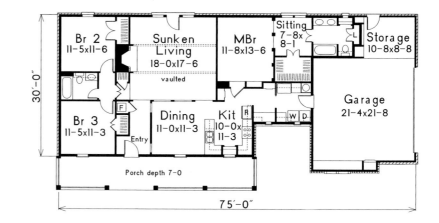

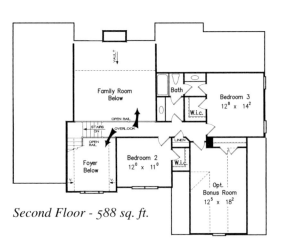

Second Floor - 588 sq. ft.

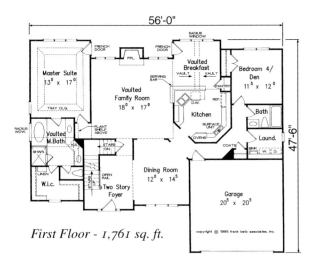

First Floor - 1,761 sq. ft.

Plan #587-035D-0029

Total Square Feet - 2,349
Bedrooms - 4
Baths - 3
Garage - 2-car

Foundation - Walk-out basement, slab or crawl space, please specify when ordering

This open and airy home features a two-story foyer and family room. The possibility of a home office can become a reality with the den secluded from the rest of the home making an ideal office space. Also, all the second floor bedrooms have walk-in closets and share a bath for maximum efficiency and organization. The optional bonus room has an additional 276 square feet of living area perfect for casual family relaxation.

Price Code D

Plan #587-038D-0018

Total Square Feet - 1,792

Bedrooms - 3

Baths - 2

Garage - 2-car drive under

Foundation - Basement

Special decorative details really add something to the interior. Decorative beams and sloped ceilings add interest to the kitchen, living and dining rooms. While a central stone fireplace and windows on two walls are focal points in the living room. Enjoy a master bedroom adorned with a private bath and large walk-in closet.

Price Code B

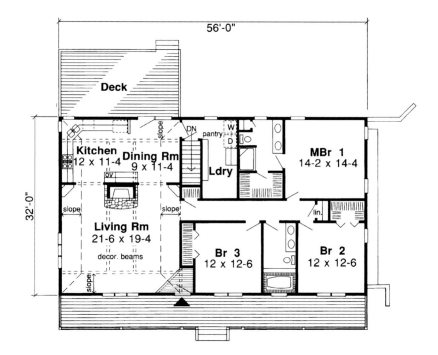

56'-0"

32'-0"

Deck

Kitchen
12 x 11-4

Dining Rm
9 x 11-4

DN

pantry

W
D

Ldry

MBr 1
14-2 x 14-4

slope

slope

slope

Living Rm
21-6 x 19-4

decor. beams

slope

Br 3
12 x 12-6

lin.

Br 2
12 x 12-6

Rear View

Second Floor - 905 sq. ft.

Total Square Feet - 1,998

Bedrooms - 3

Baths - 2 1/2

Garage - 2-car

Foundation - Basement

*A lovely designed family room
offers a double-door entrance into
the living area. Or, step inside
a roomy kitchen with a breakfast
area that is bound to be a gathering
place. A spacious atmosphere
is easily achieved in the master
bedroom with a 10' ceiling.*

Price Code C

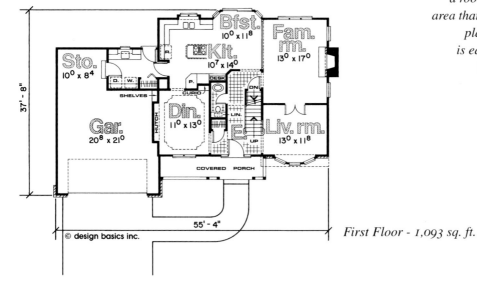

First Floor - 1,093 sq. ft.

Plan #587-021D-0016

Total Square Feet - 1,600

Bedrooms - 3

Baths - 2

Garage - 2-car side entry

Foundation - Crawl space, drawings also include slab

This energy efficient home offers 2" x 6" exterior walls for conserving energy during the hot summers and cold winter months. Inside, the first floor master bedroom is accessible from two points of entry. Plus, the master bath dressing area includes separate vanities and a mirrored makeup counter adding a touch of elegance and luxury to the space. All the second floor bedrooms have generous storage space and share a full bath.

Price Code B

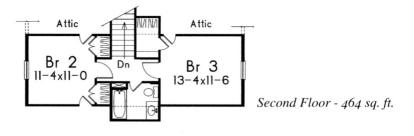

Second Floor - 464 sq. ft.

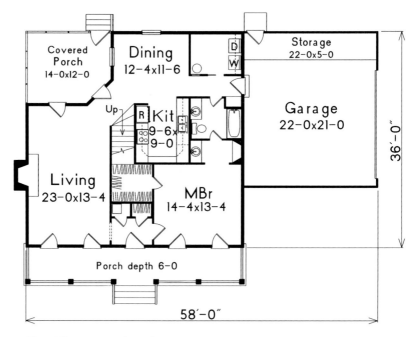

First Floor - 1,136 sq. ft.

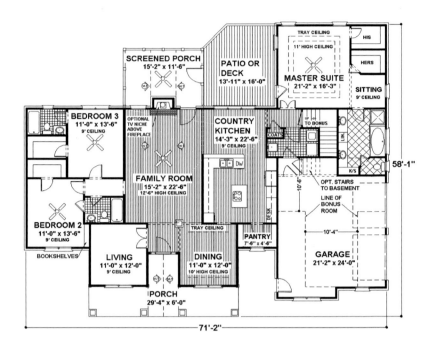

Total Square Feet - 2,184

Bedrooms - 3

Baths - 3

Garage - 2-car side entry

Foundation - Basement, crawl space or slab, please specify when ordering

This home offers a great transition from the indoor to the outdoor living areas. The delightful family room has access to the screened porch for enjoyable outdoor experiences. Also included, a formal living room has a double-door entry easily converting it to a study or home office. Regarding the bedrooms, the secluded master suite is complete with a sitting area and luxurious bath while the two secondary bedrooms share a full bath. A bonus room above the garage has an additional 379 square feet of living space perfect for expansion when necessary.

Price Code C

Plan #587-052D-0032

Total Square Feet - 1,765

Bedrooms - 3

Baths - 2 1/2

Garage - 2-car drive under

Foundation - Basement

A palladian window accenting the stone gable adds a new look to a popular cottage design exterior seen here. Inside, the dormers above open the vaulted living room in a creative and old-fashioned way. Enter the kitchen and find the breakfast room with access to a sundeck perfect for casual dining and seasonal entertaining.

Price Code B

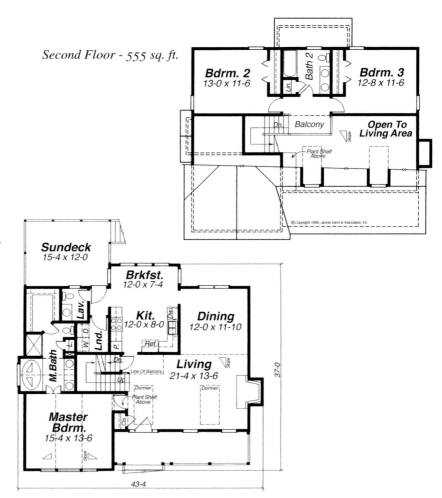

Second Floor - 555 sq. ft.

First Floor - 1,210 sq. ft.

FUTURE SPACE

4' WALL

8' LINE

BONUS ROOM
21'-10" X 13'-2"

DN

BATH

ATTIC STORAGE

Optional Second Floor - 367 sq. ft.

66' 0"

PATIO

WHP TUB

M. BATH
16'-8" X 11'-6"

BED RM. 4
14'-4" X 11'-0"

COVERED GRILLING
PORCH
31'-8" X 9'-0"

MASTER
BEDROOM
16'-8" X 14'-0"
9' BOXED CEILING

BRKFST. RM.
12'-6" X 9'-6"

LIN

BATH

GREAT RM.
19'-6" X 17'-0"
18' CEILING

KITCHEN
12'-6" X 10'-0"

REF   PAN

CT

B

LAUNDRY
7'-6" X 8'-8"
W   D

1/2 B.

65' 2"

LIN

BUILT-INS
(OPT. TO STUDY)

OVEN

DW

UP   OR   DN

BED RM. 3
10'-6" X 12'-0"

OPT.
DOOR

FOYER
18' CEILING

DINING RM.
11'-0" X 14'-4"
11' BOXED
CEILING

GARAGE
20'-4" X 22'-10"

BED RM. 2 /
STUDY
11'-0" X 12'-0"

COVERED PORCH

OPTIONAL FRONT GARAGE

© 2001 NELSON DESIGN GROUP, LLC.

First Floor - 2,261 sq. ft.

Plan #587-055D-0088

Total Square Feet - 2,261

Bedrooms - 4

Baths - 3 1/2

Garage - 2-car side entry

*Foundation - Slab or crawl space,
please specify when ordering*

*The efficiently designed
kitchen features a work island and
snack bar. Just beyond, the
spacious laundry room includes
workspace and a fold-down ironing
board maximizing efficiency.
Luxury is enjoyed by the master
bedroom and bath featuring a double
vanity, whirlpool tub and two walk-in
closets. The optional
second floor has an additional
367 square feet of living area
perfect for future expansion.*

Price Code D

Plan #587-048D-0008

Total Square Feet - 2,089

Bedrooms - 4
Baths - 3
Garage - 2-car
Foundation - Slab

The family room features a fireplace, built-in bookshelves and triple sliders opening to the covered patio. A quality kitchen overlooks the family room and features a pantry and desk for optimum organization. With regards to the more private areas, the three secondary bedrooms are separated from the master bedroom allowing a quiet retreat with patio access and also featuring an oversized bath with a walk-in closet and corner tub.

Price Code C

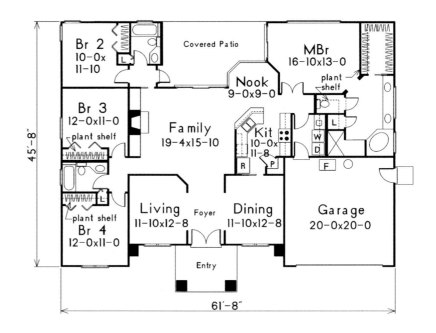

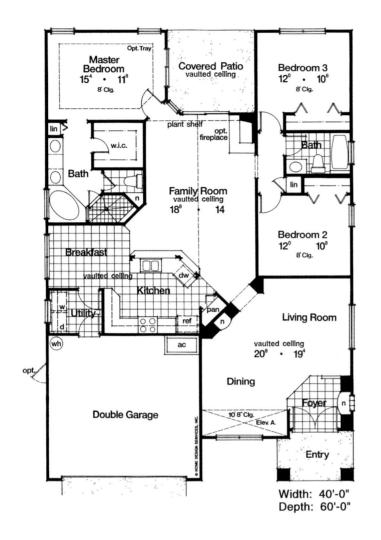

Plan #587-047D-0022

Total Square Feet - 1,768

Bedrooms - 3
Baths - 2
Garage - 2-car
Foundation - Slab

Uniquely designed vaulted living and dining rooms combine making great use of space and adding an overall spacious feeling to this home. In addition, the informal family room has a vaulted ceiling, plant shelf accents and a kitchen overlook contributing to this open feeling. A sunny breakfast area conveniently accesses the kitchen.

Price Code B

Width: 40'-0"
Depth: 60'-0"

Plan #587-011D-0010

Total Square Feet - 2,197

Bedrooms - 3
Baths - 2 1/2
Garage - 3-car
Foundation - Crawl space

A centrally located great room opens to the kitchen, breakfast nook and private backyard perfect for family style barbecues. Remaining more private, the den located off the entry is ideal for a home office. Or, pamper yourself in the vaulted master bath featuring a spa tub, shower and double vanity.

Price Code C

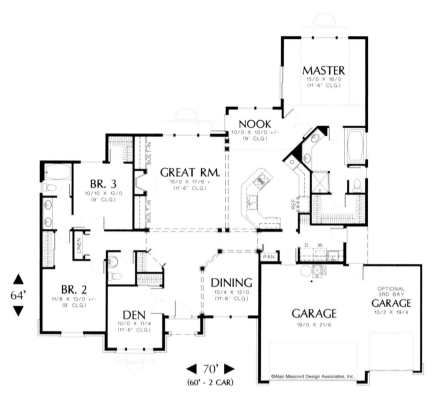

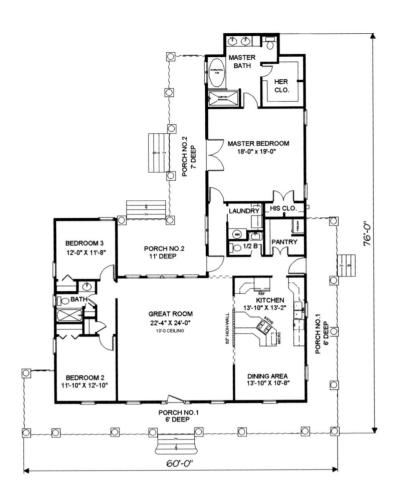

Total Square Feet - 2,123
Bedrooms - 3
Baths - 2 1/2
Foundation - Crawl space or slab,
please specify when ordering

The L-shaped porch extends the
entire length of this home creating
plenty of extra space for outdoor
living. Inside, the efficiently designed
kitchen offers an extended counter for
casual meals and lots of workspace.
A lovely master bedroom is secluded
for privacy and has two closets, a
double vanity in the bath and
a double-door entry onto the
covered porch.

Price Code C

Plan #587-053D-0017

Total Square Feet - 2,529

Bedrooms - 4

Baths - 2 1/2

Garage - 2-car

Foundation - Basement

Distinguished appearance enhances this home's classic interior arrangement. On the second floor, the master bath enjoys a garden tub, a walk-in closet and coffered ceiling decorating the master bedroom suite and creating a more luxurious surrounding. The addition of a bonus room over the garage, which is included in the square footage, has direct access from the attic and the second floor hall making the area really convenient from the rest of the home once it's been completed.

Price Code E

Second Floor - 1,410 sq. ft.

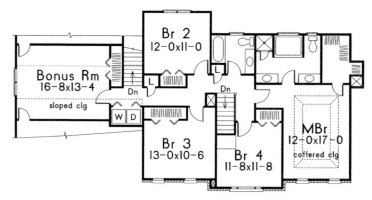

First Floor - 1,119 sq. ft.

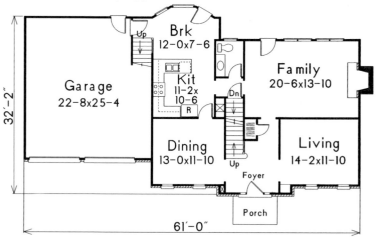

Total Square Feet - 2,534

Bedrooms - 3

Baths - 2

Garage - 3-car side entry

*Foundation - Slab or crawl space,
please specify when ordering*

*Simple elegance has been achieved
in the style and design of this home.
A large laundry room is conveniently
located adjacent to the garage
entrance and the kitchen making
household chores a breeze. Elegant
French doors lead into the study from
the spacious great room. Also, the
private master suite enjoys a 10' box
ceiling and a deluxe bath with two
vanities and walk-in closets.*

Price Code E

Plan #587-048D-0005

Total Square Feet - 2,287

Bedrooms - 4
Baths - 2 1/2
Garage - 2-car side entry
Foundation - Slab

This home features the perfect facade for Floridian style living. Upon entering, the spacious foyer opens into formal dining and living rooms. The kitchen easily serves the formal and informal areas of the home creating a perfect balance. Also impressive is the double-door entry leading into an exceptional master bedroom which accesses the covered porch and features a deluxe bath with double closets and a step-up tub.

Price Code E

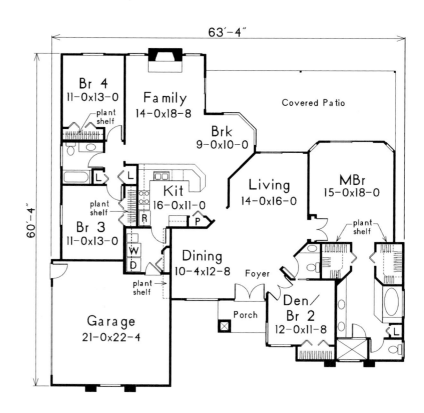

Home Plans Index

Plan Number	Square Feet	Price Code	Page	Material List	Right Read. Reverse	Can. Shipping
587-001D-0007	2,874	E	196	•		
587-001D-0013	1,882	D	154	•		
587-001D-0024	1,360	A	110	•		
587-001D-0031	1,501	B	107	•		
587-001D-0036	1,320	A	151	•		
587-001D-0040	864	AAA	157	•		
587-001D-0067	1,285	B	129	•		
587-001D-0074	1,664	B	143	•		
587-001D-0086	1,154	AA	178	•		
587-003D-0005	1,708	B	117	•		
587-004D-0001	2,505	D	153	•		
587-004D-0002	1,823	C	140	•		
587-005D-0001	1,400	B	108	•		
587-006D-0002	3,222	F	137	•		
587-006D-0003	1,674	B	176	•		
587-007D-0001	2,597	E	183	•		
587-007D-0002	3,814	G	207	•		
587-007D-0007	2,523	D	10	•		
587-007D-0008	2,452	D	139	•		
587-007D-0010	1,721	C	6	•		
587-007D-0015	2,828	F	125	•		
587-007D-0016	3,850	F	193	•		
587-007D-0017	1,882	C	128	•		
587-007D-0030	1,140	AA	156	•		
587-007D-0038	1,524	B	163	•		
587-007D-0049	1,791	C	111	•		
587-007D-0050	2,723	E	186	•		
587-007D-0054	1,575	B	133	•		
587-007D-0055	2,029	D	109	•		
587-007D-0057	2,808	F	169	•		
587-007D-0058	4,826	G	136	•		
587-007D-0060	1,268	B	113	•		
587-007D-0062	2,483	D	174	•		
587-007D-0065	2,218	D	190	•		
587-007D-0067	1,761	B	116	•		
587-007D-0068	1,384	B	120	•		
587-007D-0075	1,684	B	177	•		
587-007D-0077	1,977	C	131	•		
587-007D-0085	1,787	B	172	•		
587-007D-0089	2,125	C	148	•		
587-007D-0098	2,397	D	123	•		
587-007D-0102	1,452	A	166	•		
587-007D-0132	4,370	G	50			
587-007D-0165	3,352	F	159			
587-010D-0006	1,170	AA	135	•		
587-011D-0007	1,580	C	210	•	•	
587-011D-0010	2,197	C	228	•	•	
587-011D-0021	1,464	C	191	•	•	
587-011D-0046	2,277	E	182	•	•	
587-011D-0047	2,120	E	216	•	•	
587-013D-0001	1,050	AA	195	•		
587-013D-0015	1,787	B	119		•	
587-013D-0019	1,992	C	171	•	•	
587-013D-0022	1,992	C	106	•	•	
587-013D-0025	2,097	C	211	•	•	
587-013D-0027	2,184	C	223	•	•	
587-016D-0045	2,696	F	26	•		
587-016D-0046	2,796	F	48	•		
587-016D-0047	1,860	D	66	•		
587-016D-0049	1,793	B	8	•		
587-016D-0050	2,470	F	94	•		
587-016D-0058	2,874	G	34	•		
587-016D-0064	4,027	H	78	•		
587-016D-0065	2,585	D	84	•		
587-017D-0007	1,567	C	212	•		
587-020D-0007	1,828	C	16			
587-020D-0013	3,012	E	155			
587-020D-0015	1,191	AA	150			
587-021D-0001	2,396	D	175	•		
587-021D-0006	1,600	C	218	•		
587-021D-0012	1,672	C	202	•		
587-021D-0016	1,600	B	222	•		
587-021D-0020	2,360	D	213	•		
587-023D-0002	2,869	E	68	•		
587-024D-0008	1,650	B	46			
587-024D-0024	2,481	D	230			
587-024D-0042	1,880	C	52			
587-024D-0047	2,205	C	92			
587-024D-0048	2,240	H	28			
587-024D-0051	2,471	E	62			
587-024D-0055	2,968	H	104			
587-024D-0056	3,085	G	18			
587-024D-0058	3,176	G	86			
587-024D-0060	3,268	H	38			
587-024D-0061	3,335	H	80			
587-024D-0062	4,257	H	100			
587-026D-0110	1,999	C	208	•		
587-026D-0112	1,911	C	214	•	•	
587-026D-0121	2,270	D	197	•		
587-026D-0122	1,850	C	203	•	•	
587-026D-0123	1,998	C	221	•		
587-027D-0005	2,135	D	145	•		
587-027D-0006	2,076	C	161	•		
587-027D-0007	2,444	D	168	•		
587-028D-0001	864	AAA	184			•
587-028D-0004	1,785	B	170			•
587-028D-0006	1,700	B	199			
587-028D-0008	2,156	C	180			•
587-028D-0011	2,123	C	229			•
587-033D-0012	1,546	C	118	•		
587-035D-0011	1,945	C	192	•		
587-035D-0028	1,779	B	121	•		
587-035D-0029	2,349	D	219	•		
587-035D-0032	1,856	C	130	•		
587-035D-0035	2,322	D	142	•		
587-035D-0036	2,193	C	126	•		
587-035D-0040	2,126	C	147	•	•	
587-035D-0042	2,311	D	165	•		
587-035D-0045	1,749	B	115	•		
587-035D-0048	1,915	C	134	•		
587-035D-0050	1,342	A	149	•		
587-035D-0056	2,246	D	152	•		
587-038D-0008	1,738	B	209	•	•	
587-038D-0018	1,792	B	220	•		
587-038D-0039	1,771	B	217	•		
587-038D-0040	1,642	B	188	•		
587-038D-0046	4,064	G	30	•		
587-039D-0001	1,253	A	146	•		
587-040D-0001	1,833	D	162	•		
587-040D-0003	1,475	B	122	•		
587-040D-0007	2,073	D	164	•		
587-040D-0027	1,597	C	160	•		
587-047D-0019	1,783	B	201	•		
587-047D-0022	1,768	B	227	•		
587-047D-0046	2,597	D	215	•		
587-047D-0052	3,098	F	20			
587-047D-0056	3,426	F	40			
587-048D-0004	2,397	E	200	•		
587-048D-0005	2,287	E	232	•		
587-048D-0008	2,089	C	226	•		
587-048D-0011	1,550	B	127	•		
587-051D-0076	3,291	G	70			
587-051D-0116	3,511	G	54			
587-051D-0181	3,650	G	88			
587-051D-0182	2,600	F	96			
587-051D-0186	3,489	G	36			
587-051D-0188	3,909	G	102			
587-052D-0019	1,532	B	22			
587-052D-0032	1,765	B	224			
587-052D-0115	3,011	F	64	•		
587-052D-0121	3,223	F	72	•		
587-053D-0002	1,668	C	112	•		
587-053D-0017	2,529	E	230	•		
587-053D-0029	1,220	A	141	•		
587-053D-0030	1,657	B	132	•		
587-053D-0032	1,404	A	173	•		
587-053D-0053	1,609	B	205	•		
587-055D-0017	1,525	B	114	•	•	
587-055D-0021	5,548	H	56	•	•	
587-055D-0030	2,107	C	144	•	•	
587-055D-0088	2,261	D	225	•	•	
587-055D-0131	1,461	B	206	•	•	
587-055D-0174	2,755	E	12	•	•	
587-055D-0204	2,534	E	231	•	•	
587-055D-0304	3,901	G	76	•	•	
587-055D-0350	1,451	B	42	•	•	
587-058D-0010	676	AAA	189			
587-058D-0012	1,143	AA	194	•		
587-058D-0016	1,558	B	124	•		
587-058D-0020	1,428	A	158	•		
587-058D-0021	1,477	A	198	•		
587-058D-0033	1,440	A	187	•		
587-062D-0031	1,073	AA	185	•	•	•
587-062D-0041	1,541	B	204	•	•	•
587-062D-0048	1,543	B	167	•	•	
587-062D-0050	1,408	A	138	•	•	
587-062D-0052	1,795	B	181	•	•	
587-065D-0013	2,041	C	90		•	
587-065D-0041	3,171	E	32	•	•	
587-065D-0043	3,816	F	58	•	•	
587-065D-0077	4,328	G	44	•	•	
587-065D-0078	3,421	F	82	•	•	
587-065D-0087	3,688	F	14	•	•	
587-065D-0114	4,016	D	98		•	
587-065D-0120	5,143	H	74		•	
587-071D-0003	2,890	E	24		•	
587-071D-0006	3,746	G	179		•	
587-071D-0010	5,250	H	60		•	

What's The Right Plan For You?

Many of the homes you see may appear to be just what you're looking for. But are they? One way to find out is to carefully analyze what you want in a home. This is an important first step we'll show you how to take.

For most people, budget is the most critical element in narrowing the choices. Generally, the size of the home, or, specifically, the square footage of living area is the single most important criteria in establishing the cost of a new home. Also, in most instances, it's cheaper to build up than to build out (assuming the same amount of square footage). Sprawling ranch houses have twice the foundation and roof area of the multi-level homes covering half the ground area.

Your next task is to consider the style of home you want. Should it be traditional, contemporary, one-story or two-story? If yours is an infill lot in an existing neighborhood, is the design you like compatible with the existing residential architecture? If not, will the subdivision permit you to build the design of your choice?

And what about the site itself? What will it allow you to do and what won't it allow you to do?

Site topography is the first consideration in floor plan development. Slopes, both gentle and steep, will affect the home design you select. If you want a multi-level home with a walk-out basement that appears to be a single-story residence from the street, you need a lot that slopes from front to back. And what about the garage? Do you prefer access at street level or a lower level?

Next, there is the issue of orientation, that is, the direction in which you want the house to face. Considering the north-south or east-west orientation of the site itself, will the plan you choose allow you to enjoy sweeping views from the living room? Does the design have a lot of glass on the south side that will permit you to take advantage of the sun's warmth in winter?

Now for the tough part; figuring out what you want inside the house to satisfy your needs and lifestyle. To a large extent, that may depend on where you are in life – just starting out, whether you have toddlers or teenagers, whether you're an "empty-nester," or retired.

Next, think about the components of the home. Do you want, or need, both a living room and family room or would just one large great room suffice? Do you want, or need, both a breakfast room and a formal dining room? How many bedrooms, full baths and half baths do you need? How much storage? And what about space for working from home, hobbies or a workshop?

When you've completed your wish list, think about how you want your home to function. In architectural terms, think about spatial relationships and circulation, or in other words, the relationship of each of the components to one another.

For example, to deliver groceries conveniently, the kitchen should be directly accessible from the garage. To serve meals efficiently, the dining area should be adjacent to the kitchen. The same principle applies to other areas and components of the home. Consider the flow from entry foyer to living, sleeping, and food preparation areas.

> *Experts in the field suggest that the best way to determine your needs is to begin by listing everything you like or dislike about your current home.*

As you study your favorite home plan, ask yourself if it's possible to close off certain spaces to eliminate noise from encroaching upon others. For instance, if you enjoy listening to music, you don't want it drowned out by a droning dishwasher or blaring TV being watched by another member of the family nearby. Similarly, sleeping areas and bathrooms should be remote from living areas. After you've come to terms with the types and relationship of rooms you want in your dream home, you can then concentrate on the size and features you want for each of those spaces.

If cooking is a hobby and you entertain frequently, you might want a large gourmet kitchen or even the ever-so-popular outdoor kitchen. If you like openness and a laid-back environment, you might want a large family room with picture windows, a fireplace, vaulted ceiling, and exposed wood beams. A central living area directly accessible to an outdoor deck or patio is the ultimate in casual, relaxed style.

Deciding what you want in your dream home, where you want it, and how you want it to look is thought provoking and time consuming, but careful planning and thought will have a great return on investment when it comes to you and your family's happiness.

What Kind Of Plan Package Do You Need?

Now that you've found the home you've been looking for, here are some suggestions on how to make your Dream Home a reality. To get started, order the type of plans that fit your particular situation.

Your Choices

The One-Set Study Package -

We offer a One-set plan package so you can study your home in detail. This one set is considered a study set and is marked "not for construction." It is a copyright violation to reproduce blueprints.

The Minimum 5-Set Package -

If you're ready to start the construction process, this 5-set package is the minimum number of blueprint sets you will need. It will require keeping close track of each set so they can be used by multiple subcontractors and tradespeople.

The Standard 8-Set Package -

For best results in terms of cost, schedule and quality of construction, we recommend you order eight (or more) sets of blueprints. Besides one set for yourself, additional sets of blueprints will be required by your mortgage lender, local building department, general contractor and all subcontractors working on foundation, electrical, plumbing, heating/air conditioning, carpentry work, etc.

Reproducible Masters -

If you wish to make some minor design changes, you'll want to order reproducible masters. These drawings contain the same information as the blueprints but are printed on erasable and reproducible paper which clearly indicates your right to copy or reproduce. This will allow your builder or a local design professional to make the necessary drawing changes without the major expense of redrawing the plans. This package also allows you to print copies of the modified plans as needed. The right of building only one structure from these plans is licensed exclusively to the buyer. You may not use this design to build a second or multiple dwelling(s) without purchasing another blueprint. Each violation of the Copyright Law is punishable in a fine.

Mirror Reverse Sets -

Plans can be printed in mirror reverse. These plans are useful when the house would fit your site better if all the rooms were on the opposite side than shown. They are simply a mirror image of the original drawings causing the lettering and dimensions to read backwards. Therefore, when ordering mirror reverse drawings, you must purchase at least one set of right-reading plans. Some of our plans are offered mirror reverse right-reading. This means the plan, lettering and dimensions are flipped but read correctly. See the Home Plans Index on page 233 for availability.

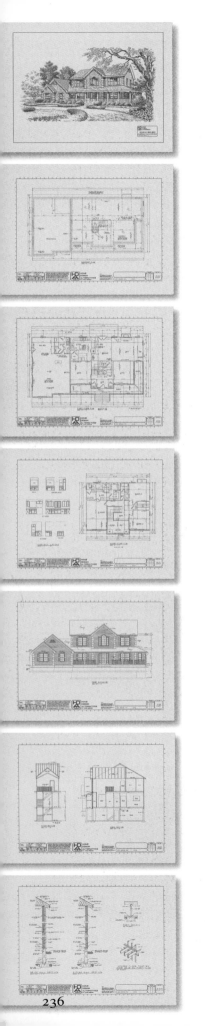

Our Blueprint Packages Offer...

Quality plans for building your future, with extras that provide unsurpassed value, ensure good construction and long-term enjoyment.

1. Cover Sheet

Included with many of the plans, the cover sheet is the artist's rendering of the exterior of the home. It will give you an idea of how your home will look when completed and landscaped.

2. Foundation

The foundation plan shows the layout of the basement, walk-out basement, crawl space, slab or pier foundation. All necessary notations and dimensions are included. See plan page for the foundation types included. If the home plan you choose does not have your desired foundation type, our Customer Service Representatives can advise you on how to customize your foundation to suit your specific needs or site conditions.

3. Floor Plans

The floor plans show the placement of walls, doors, closets, plumbing fixtures, electrical outlets, columns, and beams for each level of the home.

4. Interior Elevations

Interior elevations provide views of special interior elements such as fireplaces, kitchen cabinets, built-in units and other features of the home.

5. Exterior Elevations

Exterior elevations illustrate the front, rear and both sides of the house, with all details of exterior materials and the required dimensions.

6. Sections

Show detail views of the home or portions of the home as if it were sliced from the roof to the foundation. This sheet shows important areas such as load-bearing walls, stairs, joists, trusses and other structural elements, which are critical for proper construction.

7. Details

Show how to construct certain components of your home, such as the roof system, stairs, deck, etc.

Making Changes To Your Plan

We understand that it is difficult to find blueprints for a home that will meet all your needs. That is why HDA, Inc. (Home Design Alternatives) is pleased to offer home plan modification services.

Typical home plan modifications include:

- Changing foundation type
- Adding square footage to a plan
- Changing the entry into a garage
- Changing a two-car garage to a three-car garage or making a garage larger
- Redesigning kitchen, baths, and bedrooms
- Changing exterior elevations
- Or most other home plan modifications you may desire!

Some home plan modifications we cannot make include:

- Reversing the plans
- Adapting/engineering plans to meet your local building codes
- Combining parts of two different plans (due to copyright laws)

Our plan modification service is easy to use. Simply:

1. Decide on the modifications you want. For the most accurate quote, be as detailed as possible and refer to rooms in the same manner as the floor plan (i.e. if the floor plan refers to a "den", then use "den" in your description). Including a sketch of the modified floor plan is always helpful.

2. Complete and e-mail the modification request form that can be found online at www.houseplansandmore.com.

3. Within two business days, you will receive your quote. Quotes do not include the cost of the reproducible masters required for our designer to legally make changes.

4. Call to accept the quote and purchase the reproducible masters. For example, if your quote is $850 and the reproducible masters for your plan are $800, your order total will be $1650 plus two shipping and handling charges (one to ship the reproducible masters to our designer and one to ship the modified plans to you).

5. Our designer will send you up to three drafts to verify your initial changes. Extra costs apply after the third draft. If additional changes are made that alter the original request, extra charges may be incurred.

6. Once you approve a draft with the final changes, we then make the changes to the reproducible masters by adding additional sheets. The original reproducible masters (with no changes) plus your new changed sheets will be shipped to you.

Other Important Information:

- Plans cannot be redrawn in reverse format. All modifications will be made to match the reproducible master's original layout. Once you receive the plans, you can make reverse copies at your local blueprint shop.

- Our staff designer will provide the first draft for your review within 4 weeks (plus shipping time) of receiving your order.

- You will receive up to three drafts to review before your original changes are modified. The first draft will totally encompass all modifications based on your original request. Additional changes not included in your original request will be charged separately at an hourly rate of $75 or a flat quoted rate.

- Modifications will be drawn on a separate sheet with the changes shown and a note to see the main sheet for details. For example, a floor plan sheet from the original set (i.e. Sheet 3) would be followed by a new floor plan sheet with changes (i.e. Sheet A-3).

- Plans are drawn to meet national building codes. Modifications will not be drawn to any particular state or county codes, thus we cannot guarantee that the revisions will meet your local building codes. You may be required to have a local architect or designer review the plans in order to have them comply with your state or county building codes.

- Time and cost estimates are good for 90 calendar days.

- All modification requests need to be submitted in writing. Verbal requests will not be accepted.

---

2 Easy Steps for FAST service

1. Visit www.houseplansandmore.com to download the modification request form.

2. E-mail the completed form to customize@hdainc.com or fax to 913-856-7751

If you are not able to access the internet, please call 1-800-373-2646 (Monday-Friday, 8am-5pm CST)

More Helpful Building Aids

Your Blueprint Package will contain the necessary construction information to build your home. We also offer the following products and services to save you time and money in the building process.

Material List

Material lists are available for many of the plans in this book. Each list gives you the quantity, dimensions and description of the building materials necessary to construct your home. You'll get faster and more accurate bids from your contractor while saving money by paying for only the materials you need. See the Home Plans Index on page 233 for availability. Cost: $125.00

Note: Material lists are not refundable.

Express Delivery

Most orders are processed within 24 hours of receipt. Please allow 7-10 business days for delivery. If you need to place a rush order, please call us by 11:00 a.m. Monday-Friday CST and ask for express service (allow 1-2 business days).

Technical Assistance

If you have questions, call our technical support line at 1-314-770-2228 between 8:00 a.m. and 5:00 p.m. Monday-Friday CST. Whether it involves design modifications or field assistance, our designers are extremely familiar with all of our designs and will be happy to help you. We want your home to be everything you expect it to be.

Other Great Products...

The Legal Kit -

Avoid many legal pitfalls and build your home with confidence using the forms and contract featured in this kit. Included are request for proposal documents, various fixed price and cost plus contracts, instructions on how and when to use each form, warranty statements and more. Save time and money before you break ground on your new home or start a remodeling project. All forms are reproducible. The kit is ideal for homebuilders and contractors. Cost: $35.00

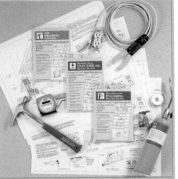

Detail Plan Packages -
Electrical, Plumbing and Framing Packages -

Three separate packages offer homebuilders details for constructing various foundations; numerous floor, wall and roof framing techniques; simple to complex residential wiring; sump and water softener hookups; plumbing connection methods; installation of septic systems, and more. Each package includes three dimensional illustrations and a glossary of terms. Purchase one or all three. Note: These drawings do not pertain to a specific home plan. Cost: $20.00 each or all three for $40.00

Before You Order

Exchange Policies

Since blueprints are printed in response to your order, we cannot honor requests for refunds. However, if for some reason you find that the plan you have purchased does not meet your requirements, you may exchange that plan for another plan in our collection within 90 days of purchase. At the time of the exchange, you will be charged a processing fee of 25% of your original plan package price, plus the difference in price between the plan packages (if applicable) and the cost to ship the new plans to you. *Please note: Reproducible drawings can only be exchanged if the package is unopened.*

Building Codes & Requirements

At the time the construction drawings were prepared, every effort was made to ensure that these plans and specifications meet nationally recognized codes. Our plans conform to most national building codes. Because building codes vary from area to area, some drawing modifications and/or the assistance of a professional designer or architect may be necessary to comply with your local codes or to accommodate specific building site conditions. We advise you to consult with your local building official for information regarding codes governing your area.

Additional Sets†

Additional sets of the plan ordered are available for an additional cost of $45.00 each. Five-set, eight-set, and reproducible packages offer considerable savings.

Mirror Reverse Plans†

Available for an additional $15.00 per set, these plans are simply a mirror image of the original drawings causing the dimensions and lettering to read backwards. Therefore, when ordering mirror reverse plans, you must purchase at least one set of right-reading plans. Some of our plans are offered mirror reverse right-reading. This means the plan, lettering and dimensions are flipped but read correctly. To purchase a mirror reverse right-reading set, the cost is an additional $150.00. See the Home Plans Index on page 233 for availability.

One-Set Study Package

We offer a one-set plan package so you can study your home in detail. This one set is considered a study set and is marked "not for construction." It is a copyright violation to reproduce blueprints.

Blueprint Price Schedule

BEST VALUE

Price Code	1-Set	5-Sets (Save $110)	8-Sets (Save $200)	Reproducible Masters
AAA	$225	$295	$340	$440
AA	$325	$395	$440	$540
A	$385	$455	$500	$600
B	$445	$515	$560	$660
C	$500	$570	$615	$715
D	$560	$630	$675	$775
E	$620	$690	$735	$835
F	$675	$745	$790	$890
G	$765	$835	$880	$980
H	$890	$960	$1005	$1105

Plan prices are subject to change without notice.
Please note that plans and material lists are not refundable.

†Available only within 90 days after purchase of plan package or reproducible masters of same plan.

Shipping & Handling Charges

U.S. Shipping - (AK and HI express only)	1-4 Sets	5-7 Sets	8 Sets or Reproducibles
Regular (allow 7-10 business days)	$15.00	$17.50	$25.00
Priority (allow 3-5 business days)	$25.00	$30.00	$35.00
Express* (allow 1-2 business days)	$35.00	$40.00	$45.00

Canada Shipping (to/from)* - Plans with suffix 062D - see index

	1-4 Sets	5-7 Sets	8 Sets or Reproducibles
Standard (allow 8-12 business days)	$35.00	$40.00	$45.00
Express* (allow 3-5 business days)	$60.00	$70.00	$80.00

Overseas Shipping/International -

Call, fax, or e-mail (plans@hdainc.com) for shipping costs.
* For express delivery please call us by 11:00 a.m. Monday-Friday CST
** Orders may be subject to custom's fee and/or duties/taxes.

Questions? Call Our Customer Service Number
1-314-770-2228

How To Order

1.) **Call** toll-free 1-800-373-2646 for credit card orders. Mastercard, Visa, Discover and American Express are accepted.

2.) **Fax** your order to 1-314-770-2226.

3.) **Mail** *t*he Order Form to: **HDA, Inc.**
    944 Anglum Road
    St. Louis, MO 63042

4.) **Online** visit www.houseplansandmore.com

For fastest service, Call Toll-Free
1-800-DREAM HOME (1-800-373-2646) day or night

Order Form

Please send me -

PLAN NUMBER 587- _____

　　　　　PRICE CODE _____ *(see page 233)*

Specify Foundation Type *(see plan page for availability)*

☐ Slab ☐ Crawl space ☐ Pier

☐ Basement ☐ Walk-out basement

☐ Reproducible Masters $_____

☐ Eight-Set Plan Package $_____

☐ Five-Set Plan Package $_____

☐ One-Set Study Package *(no mirror reverse)* $_____

Additional Plan Sets† *(see page 239)*

　　☐ ____ (Qty.) at $45.00 each $_____

Mirror Reverse† *(see page 239)*

　　☐ Right-reading $150 one-time charge
　　　 (see index on page 233 for availability) $_____

　　☐ Print in Mirror Reverse
　　　 (where right-reading is not available)
　　　 ____ (Qty.) at $15.00 each $_____

☐ Material List† $125 *(see page 233 for availability)*
　 (see page 239 for more information) $_____

☐ Legal Kit *(002D-9991, see page 238)* $_____

Detail Plan Packages: *(see page 238)*

　　☐ Framing ☐ Electrical ☐ Plumbing
　　(002D-9992) (002D-9993) (002D-9994)
　　　　　　　　　　　　　　　　　　　　$_____   4

　　　　　　SUBTOTAL $_____

Sales Tax *(MO residents add 6%)* $_____

☐ Shipping / Handling *(see chart at right)* $_____

TOTAL *(US funds only - sorry no CODs)* $_____

I hereby authorize HDA, Inc. to charge this purchase to my credit card account (check one):

☐ MasterCard   ☐ VISA   ☐ DISCOVER   ☐ AMERICAN EXPRESS Cards

Plan prices are subject to change without notice.
Please note that plans and material lists are not refundable.

Credit Card number_____

Expiration date _____

Signature _____

Name_____
　　　　　　　(Please print or type)

Street Address _____
　　　　　　　(Please do not use a PO Box)

_____

City _____

State_____

Zip_____

Daytime phone number (_____) -_____

E-mail address_____

I am a ☐ Builder/Contractor
　　　　☐ Homeowner
　　　　☐ Renter

I ☐ have ☐ have not selected my general contractor.

Thank you for your order!